The Dangers
of Passion

The Dangers *of* Passion

*The Transcendental Friendship
of Ralph Waldo Emerson
& Margaret Fuller*

by Daniel Bullen

Copyright © 2012 by Daniel Bullen

Published by Levellers Press
Amherst, Massachusetts

ISBN 978-1-937146-08-5

again, to Meaghan

I will have no covenants but proximities. I shall endeavour to nourish my parents, to support my family, to be the chaste husband of one wife,—but these relations I must fill after a new and unprecedented way.

Ralph Waldo Emerson, "Self-Reliance"

No old [form] suits me. If I could invent one, it seems to me the pleasure of creation would make it possible for me to write…I want force to be either a genius or a character. One should be either private or public. I love best to be a woman; but womanhood is at present too straitly-bounded to give me scope. At hours, I live truly as a woman; at others, I should stifle; as, on the other hand, I should palsy, when I would play the artist.

Margaret Fuller to Sam Ward

I

WHEN MARGARET FULLER OSSOLI DROWNED IN A SHIPWRECK off the coast of Long Island in 1850, she was in the middle of her career. She had gone to Europe as a correspondent for the *Herald Tribune*, but she had not simply reported on the Italian Revolution of 1848: she married and had a child by an Italian Count who was active in the movement, and when Rome was besieged by the Pope's French troops, she helped run a hospital until the movement to unify Italy was defeated. As her ship approached the American coast, she had only been married for about a year, and she was returning to the U.S. with her new husband and infant child after having spent four years in Europe.

Before leaving for Europe, Fuller had written two books about women's lives in modern times, and everyone who knew her—everyone who had an opinion about a woman's role in American society—was curious to see whether this feminist writer and intellectual had been domesticated by marriage and childbirth. When she had written home with the first news of her marriage, though, she had withheld so many details that even her close friends were uncertain about her new marriage. Now that she was coming back, they wondered whether she had discovered a new kind of husband: would Ossoli allow his wife to be the intellectual 'head of the house'? The news that he was a Catholic, and poorly-educated, was more puzzling than encouraging, but Fuller and Ossoli never got to answer the questions people had about their marriage. Their ship was caught in a hurricane off of Long Island, and when it struck a sand bar, the cargo of marble burst through the hull and the ship broke up in the surf.

In the intense public interest that followed her death, three of Fuller's good friends became her biographers and editors. None of them had seen her since she left America four years earlier—and none of them had met her husband, or knew much about her life in Italy—but Ralph Waldo Emerson, James Freeman Clarke and William Channing nonetheless sifted through her journals, letters and manuscripts, and pieced her words together with friends' reflections to make *The Memoirs of Margaret Fuller Ossoli*, which was published in 1852. *The Memoirs'* portrait of Fuller was largely laudatory, but its praises tended toward Horace Greeley's view of an exceptional woman whom "a good husband and two or three bouncing babies would have emancipated…from a good deal of cant and nonsense." It would seem that America was simply not ready to accept an intellectual woman who expected to have a writing career even after she married.

But there was a personal element in the *Memoirs'* faintly damning praises. Emerson was seven years older than Fuller, and when they met in 1836, he had already begun to make a name for himself with essays and lectures on the subject of the modern American freedoms. His ideas about self-reliance were becoming attractive to an American culture that was throwing off European influences as it expanded Westward and developed its own unique character. Emerson would have the satisfaction of watching his ideas inspire experiments in living, as George Ripley and others founded the utopian community at Brook Farm, in 1841—and as Henry David Thoreau moved to Walden Pond for two years in 1845—but even by the time he met Fuller in 1836, his ideas were already being taken up by men and women who would become prominent educators and legislators, activists and artists. When Emerson encouraged Fuller to inquire into her own nature and to follow her own intuitions, she took his advice personally: not only did she apply his advice in her own work and in her relationships, but she challenged Emerson to live by his own philosophy.

Margaret Fuller was uniquely positioned to apply Emerson's philosophy of self-trust—not only in her essays, but in her own life. In 1836, Fuller was twenty-six years old, and she had been struggling with the question of what she would make of herself. From an early age, Fuller had received a singular education—her father had tutored her himself, so that she was reading and writing in Latin by age six—and her intelligence and her rigor of mind had set her apart from her female contemporaries. By the time she was in her twenties, Fuller was searching less for a husband than for "an intellectual guide"—someone who could love her because of—or even in spite of—her "masculine mind." When she met Emerson, she believed that she had met the person who could "discern the law by which I am filling my circle."

Emerson was not in a position to do more than encourage Fuller, though. He himself had followed his internal lights in making his first marriage, to Ellen Tucker, in September of 1829. He had loved Ellen deeply, and when she died of tuberculosis seventeen months later, he had been compensated for his devastating grief with the vision of a self-reliance that gave him confidence in himself "in spite of real sorrows." He had had his experience: he would marry again—to Lydia Jackson, a year before he met Fuller—but he would describe his second marriage as a "sober joy." Deeply impressed as he was with Fuller's mind and her personality, he had a wife, a secure income, an international reputation, and, by 1841, three small children: he was not in a position to test his theories of self-invention within his own marriage.

If Emerson himself was happily married, Fuller had still come to question—as anyone reading Emerson's essays must—whether marriage was just another obsolete institution for self-reliant people—whether the heart itself might really be the only authority on which matrimonial bonds could be forged. The intimacy that existed between Emerson and Fuller was not something we would call an affair, in the modern sense of a sexual relationship outside of marriage. But their friendship—consisting, as it did, of a married man offering personal encouragement to an unmarried, younger woman—was not strictly literary and philosophical either: it was complicated by the tensions that will arise any time a young woman reaches a degree of deep intimacy with a married man.

From 1836 to 1841, Emerson's most rhapsodic letters were written to Fuller—and in her letters and journals, Fuller more than once describes herself as the best person to lead Emerson to the fulfillment of his own philosophy—but they would part company after quarreling over precisely what kind of intimacy they could expect from each other. In lengthy letters and journal entries on the topic of their friendship, Emerson and Fuller were both deeply modern, in how they defined their obligations to their own self-fulfillment. After they parted, Fuller would go on to test her freedom in her own life—in her departure to Europe as much as in her marriage, in her writing as much as in her return to America.

With the publication of *The Memoirs of Margaret Fuller Ossoli*, Emerson presented a sanitized version of their relationship on the national stage, and even in spite of its patronizing tone and its distortions, *The Memoirs* went through thirteen printings by 1860. Two generations after the Revolution, Americans were beginning to adapt to—and of course react against—the freedoms that we think of as characteristically modern: the freedom to make ties based on talents and affinities, more than on tradition, family or religion.

The 1840s may still have been too conservative for real innovations within the bond of marriage, but the creative and rebellious self-trust that would blossom in the 1890s, and again in the 1920s and '30s—and then again in the 1960s—was already coming into view. When subsequent generations would ask themselves how to reconcile individual freedom, desire and creativity with the institution of marriage, they would be echoing Emerson and Fuller in their sense of obligation to their own freedom, and also in their private complaints about marriage's limitations. As society's authority diminished over the next hundred and fifty years—and as individuals followed Emerson's injunction to "enjoy an original relation to the universe"—it was not uncommon for spouses to use the language of self-reliance as they made marriages based on their own personal visions—as they broke from them when their hearts required freedom—and as they proposed alternatives to the lifelong monogamous tie.

II

WHEN SHE LOOKED BACK OVER HER EARLY YEARS at age thirty, Fuller wrote that "I had no natural childhood." As a young girl, her father had designed an ambitious curriculum for her, and schooled her thoroughly in classical languages and literature. It was extremely rare, in the 1810s and '20s, for a woman to be so thoroughly educated, and if formal learning distinguished young Margaret from other girls, who were not educated to the same standard, it disconcerted the boys, who did not expect girls to have intellect. But Fuller's father, a Harvard-educated lawyer and Massachusetts Congressman, believed in the value of self-cultivation, and saw no reason why he should not institute it in his own family.

Timothy Fuller's people arrived in America in 1630, when yeoman Thomas Fuller emigrated from England, and strong principles ran in the family line: Fuller's grandfather was a preacher who lost his parish for preaching pacifistic opposition to the Revolution. Fuller's father was the first member of the family to graduate from college, and he entered the law in 1804, although he did not marry until 1809, after he had put his brothers through Harvard as well. Margarett Crane, his wife, was twenty years old to his thirty, and their first daughter, Sarah Margaret, was born in 1810, a year after they married. A democrat at heart, Timothy entered politics in 1814 to campaign against aristocratic merchants who sought to separate the north from the agricultural interests in the South and West. He was elected to the United States Congress in 1816 and he oversaw his children's education from Washington while Congress was in session. A Boston memorial states that he was "untiring in his industry, grudged the hours nature demands for sleep, was a fine classic scholar, and an extensive reader."

Not content to have built a prosperous and distinguished political career for himself, Timothy raised his daughter according to a Roman model of character and citizenship, which she described in an 1840 autobiographical sketch:

> Everything [about the Romans] turns your attention to what a man can become, not by yielding himself freely to impressions, not by letting nature play freely through him, but by a single thought, an earnest purpose, an indomitable will, by hardihood, self-command, and force of expression.

Timothy trained his daughter to be an orator, as he had been, not a writer. Fuller's sketch continues:

> I was taught Latin and English grammar at the same time, and began to read Latin at six years old, after which, for some years, I read it daily. In this branch of study, first by my father, and afterwards by a tutor, I was trained to quite a high degree of precision. I was expected to understand the mechanism of the language thoroughly, and in trans-

lating to give the thoughts in as few well-arranged words as possible, and without breaks or hesitation,—for with these my father had absolutely no patience.

Indeed, he demanded accuracy and clearness in everything: you must not speak, unless you can make your meaning perfectly intelligible to the person addressed; must not express a thought, unless you can give a reason for it, if required.

Fuller bore the rigorous training well, but her father was "a man of business, even in literature," and he pushed her beyond her comfort. Waiting to recite her lessons to her father at the end of his business day, her feelings, she wrote,

were kept on the stretch till the recitations were over. Thus frequently, I was sent to bed several hours too late, with nerves unnaturally stimulated. The consequence was a premature development of the brain, that made me a "youthful prodigy" by day, and by night a victim of spectral illusions, nightmare, and somnambulism, which at the time prevented the harmonious development of my bodily powers and checked my growth, while, later, they induced continual headache, weakness and nervous affections of all kinds.

In spite of the strain, this education raised Fuller's expectations above the commonplace and set her apart. Fuller wrote that her books did me good, for by them a standard was early given of sight and thought, from which I could never go back, and beneath which I cannot suffer patiently my own life or that of any friend to fall. They did me harm, too, for the child fed with meat instead of milk becomes too soon mature. Expectations and desires were thus early raised, after which I must long toil before they can be realized. How poor the scene around, how tame one's own existence, how meagre and faint every power, with these beings in my mind!

Raised into adult company with literary expectations, Fuller was not close with her peers, either:

I had no success in associating with [the local girls] beyond the mere play. Not only was I not their school-mate, but my book-life and lonely habits had given a cold aloofness to my whole expression, and veiled my manner with a hauteur which turned all hearts away…the girls supposed me really superior to themselves, and did not hate me for feeling it, but neither did they like me, nor wish to have me with them.

Fuller's mother did not shelter her first-born daughter from her husband's high expectations. Ten years younger than her husband, she was not an intellectual herself—she was closer to the domestic ideal of woman that was prevalent in the day. Fuller's brother Richard described their mother by saying that "duty was her daily food, self-sacrifice was as natural to her as self-gratification in many others." In the face of her husband's ambitious curriculum, Margarett could not teach her daughter a woman's subservient role, either, although in an act of identification with her mother, Fuller dropped her first name, Sarah, and used her middle name, her mother's name, starting at age thirteen.

Fuller was so well educated that by the time she went to boarding school in Boston, at age eleven, she outshone even the older girls. When she took first place at exams, though, they revenged themselves socially, by excluding her. By the time she was fourteen, academic distinctions were no longer sufficient consolation: it was clear that her learning was making her uncomfortable in society, and her father sent her to Miss Prescott's finishing school for girls, where she felt "rather degraded from Cicero to one and one are how many." As she described the period in another semi-autobiographical sketch, she says that she proved to be

> a strange bird…there,—a lonely swallow that could not make for itself a summer. At first, her schoolmates were captivated with her ways; her love of wild dances and sudden song, her freaks of passion and wit. She was always new, always surprising, and, for a time, charming.
>
> But, after awhile, they tired of her. She could never be depended on to join in their plans, yet she expected them to follow out hers with their whole strength.

Fuller did not adjust smoothly: she had fostered her own individuality and uniqueness so well—she had burrowed so deep into her studies—that a friend described her as "so precocious in her mental and physical developments that [at thirteen, in 1823] she passed for eighteen or twenty." She was already preparing herself for an unconventional life, and in another autobiographical sketch, from 1843, she wrote that in matters of the heart, she would be "one of those 'Whom men love not, but yet regret.'"

Having been sent away from her father's instruction to a girls finishing school, Fuller started to identify what it would take to enter into society as a woman. She realized that her father, "trained to great dexterity in artificial methods, accurate, ready, with entire command of his resources, had no belief in minds that listen, wait, receive. He had no conception of the subtle and indirect motions of imagination and feeling." In another sketch, Fuller gave her father more credit—she said that he "addressed her not as a plaything, but as a living mind...from the time she could speak and go alone"—but his ambitious example could not help her assume her role in society as a woman.

Fuller had a hard time finding women to serve as role models. Her mother had not been able to help her, and the other older women she met in Cambridge were either teachers or else the wives of Harvard professors, and they could not show her how to enter into adult society as an intellectual woman on her own—not without a supporting spouse. America in the 1820s was not ready to accept women as independent thinkers and intellectuals. The young country was experiencing a period of territorial and industrial expansion, and as machines and factories provided a new degree of leisure, women were not valued for their independence so much as they became status symbols whose 'work' was simply to submit themselves to the men in their households. By submitting, they would embody—and therefore redeem—the spiritual life which the men were surely profaning in the newly bustling factory, marketplace or office. According to what scholars have called the Cult of True Womanhood, women—upper-class women like Fuller, especially—were expected to exemplify "piety, purity, submissiveness, and domesticity." Setting women aside as paragons of virtue or as pious domestics meant effectively hobbling them as self-governing human beings, and in her 1837 book *Society in America*, British feminist Harriet Martineau saw that

> as women have none of the objects in life for which an enlarged education is considered requisite, the education is not given…Marriage is the only object left open to woman… Literature is also said to be permitted: but under what penalties and restrictions? Nothing is thus left for women but marriage.—Yes; Religion, is the reply.—Religion is a temper, not a pursuit.

THE DANGERS OF PASSION

After two years of finishing school, in 1825 Fuller moved with her family to a large house in Cambridgeport, where her father wanted to be closer to Boston society, and where Fuller herself stood a good chance of finding a place among the students and professors at Harvard. Combining "feminine receptiveness with masculine energy," Fuller gained a reputation as a learned and intimate friend—although she was regarded as an egotist outside of her circle. If her intellect prevented her friends at Harvard from seeing her as a potential spouse, she nonetheless developed a talent for bringing people out, so that Emerson wrote in the *Memoirs* that "at Cambridge she had drawn numbers of lively young men about her...[and] a circle of young women...were devoted to her."

Fuller was beginning to grow beyond the sphere her father could prepare her for, but their fortunes were still closely tied. As Fuller was beginning to enter adult society in the late 1820s, Timothy Fuller resigned his seat in Congress. He had helped John Quincy Adams win the 1824 presidential election, and now he hoped for an ambassadorship in Europe—but the appointment never materialized. To demonstrate his diplomatic skills, Timothy Fuller had hosted a lavish dinner reception and ball for President Adams, but Adams' father had died only recently, and it was still too soon for festivities. Fuller's father held the ball nonetheless, and when Adams left early, the opportunity for the ambassadorship left with him—Fuller was passed over when the appointments were made.

The Transcendental Friendship of Ralph Waldo Emerson & Margaret Fuller

Fuller's political star turned to permanent decline when Andrew Jackson defeated Adams in the 1828 election, and when Jackson was re-elected in 1832, Fuller gave up on politics altogether and moved his family to a farm in Groton, Massachusetts, forty miles northwest of Boston. This move was a deep disappointment for Fuller, who was now twenty-three years old. Instead of ascending into intellectual society, she had to keep up with her study of languages and literature at the end of long days, after teaching her younger siblings and working beside her mother, keeping house on a farm. While her father indulged his nostalgia for country living, Fuller was removed from the only society in which she could hope to be comprehended as a woman and as a thinker.

There is no explicit record in Fuller's journals or letters that she expected to marry—or not to marry, for that matter—but she did expect a great deal of passion and intimacy from her friends. Friendship in the mid-1800s was a quasi-religious state somewhat closer to romantic love than platonic affection, and it received all the sublimated passions that had been kindled by the British and German romantics, Lord Byron and Goethe, whose young characters' lust for strong feelings had elevated friendship to the level of a shared spiritual experience. Consummation was limited to raptures shared in letters and poems—marriage remained the sole forbidding gateway to full sexual intimacy—but Fuller had many passionate friendships in Boston, all of which waxed and waned on tides of shared intellectual passion. None of them promised to raise her from passion into marriage, however, and when Emerson met her in the mid-1830s, he described her as having "already beheld many times the youth, meridian, and old age of passion." Fuller herself would say in several of her letters that she had known too many disappointments at an early age to let herself hope that new friendships would last very long.

Fuller yearned not for a husband, but for a mentor who could understand and guide her. As a unique woman, who had been trained to literature and oratory—as a woman whose intellect therefore depended on an audience—she had idealized the friends who would complete her,

> beings born under the same star, and bound with us in a common destiny. These are not mere acquaintances, mere friends, but, when we meet, are sharers of our very existence. There is no separation; the same thought is given at the same moment to both,—indeed, it is born of the meeting, and would not otherwise have been called into existence at all.

Fuller's journals and letters resound with her wish for a guide: "I study much and reflect more, and feel an aching wish for some person with whom I might talk fully and openly." Isolated in Groton—isolated again, outside of the womanly sphere by her learning—Fuller had to make a place for herself in the typical American way: by breaking virgin ground, and building a career where there was no precedent.

Fuller consoled herself in Groton by reading German literature, and after Goethe died in 1832, she planned to write a biography, although when she realized that this would require a trip to Europe for research, her father hesitated to commit the money, and the trip was postponed. Fuller studied Goethe and Schiller and German Idealism nonetheless—all of which were still virtually unknown beyond the narrow circles of Harvard students and professors who had traveled to Europe—and now she had something of her own to offer to the wide circle of writers, theologians and intellectuals she was corresponding with. Fuller was translating Goethe independently of any school or classes, though—she was not studying under a teacher, herself, she was only acting as teacher to her siblings—so that even as she progressed with her work, she had to wonder where or how it would ever be appreciated outside of the circle of her friends.

Searching for personal role models, Fuller chose Goethe and other Europeans. In addition to writers like George Sand—that "large-brained Woman, and large-hearted Man," who had made herself independent as a writer—Fuller's aspirations centered on literary mentors. Starting at the age of eight—when Fuller met a beautiful and cultured British woman named Ellen Kilshaw—intimacy between older, experienced women and young initiates became a model for her expectations. With a child's sharp longing and sympathy, Fuller had felt that she and Kilshaw understood each other better than any of the adults in their company, and she continued to look for older women who could appreciate her—and whom she could inspire, in turn, with her zealous admiration.

Instead of a friend who could comprehend her, or a guide who could absorb and direct her intellectual energy, Fuller met Liza Farrar, a Harvard professor's wife, who was in her forties. Farrar was a teacher and writer herself—she would publish *The Young Lady's Friend*, an advice book for women, in 1836—and the two women struck up "an almost maternal friendship," in which Farrar "undertook to mould [Fuller] externally, to make her less abrupt, less self-asserting." It was at Farrar's house that Fuller met Harriet Martineau in 1835, when Martineau was traveling through Boston to gather research for *Society in America*. Fuller was drawn to the older feminist writer, and wrote in her journal,

> I sigh for an intellectual guide. Nothing but the sense of what God has done for me, in bringing me nearer to himself, saves me from despair...I have hoped some friend would do,—what none had ever yet done,—comprehend me wholly, mentally and morally, and enable me better to comprehend myself. I have had some hope that Miss Martineau might be this friend, but cannot yet tell. She has what I want,—vigorous reasoning powers, invention, clear views of her objects,—and she has been trained to the best means of execution. Add to this, that there are no strong intellectual sympathies between us, such as would blind her to my defects.

The Transcendental Friendship of Ralph Waldo Emerson & Margaret Fuller

Fuller impressed Farrar's British visitor, and they struck up a friendship, so that when Martineau planned to return to Europe with the Farrars at the end of summer of 1836, Fuller was invited to come along—as were her friends Sam Ward, a Harvard senior and the "favorite son of a [self-made] Boston banker," and Anna Barker, a Southerner who was a kinswoman of Farrar's. Fuller expected this trip to complete her education, for Martineau promised to introduce her in the intellectual and literary circles that would launch her career as a writer.

To Fuller's dismay, the trip did not happen. Her father died suddenly of Asiatic cholera in 1835, and he died intestate, so that for months after his death, there was uncertainty about his estate. Fuller's family urged her to go to Europe while they settled the property, but she gave up the trip. She was barred by virtue of her sex from assuming legal responsibility for her siblings or mother, but no one else was prepared to assume the burden of administering her father's estate—or of providing for the household. She was the eldest child, and she refused to leave her mother and younger siblings at the mercy of her unsympathetic Uncle Abraham, who had assumed the executorship. Even when her share of the estate was finally settled upon her months later, she still refused to meet up with Farrar and Barker and Ward in Europe, staying in Massachusetts, instead, to manage her family.

Harriet Martineau was still in Massachusetts when Fuller's father died, and before she returned to Europe, she made

Fuller one local introduction, to Ralph Waldo Emerson, whom Martineau had met in her travels through Boston. Emerson's philosophy had just taken shape in his first book, *Nature*—he was expecting it from the printer at the end of summer 1836—and Martineau suggested that he should get to know Fuller, whose praises another mutual friend, Henry Hedge, had also been singing. Fuller had been hearing about Emerson as well, and now she was drawn to him as a potential mentor. An invitation was finally arranged at Martineau's instigation, and Fuller visited Emerson and his wife at their home in Concord for three weeks in July of 1836.

III

IN 1836, AT AGE THIRTY-THREE, WALDO EMERSON (as he had been known since college) was just starting to make a name for himself as a philosopher and writer. He had been groomed for the pulpit from an early age, and had served as a minister in Boston for four years before he broke with the church in 1832 to follow a career as a writer. He was still a religious thinker—his ideas about self-reliance and individual spiritual experience retained a ministerial authority—but when he met Fuller, his writing was defining the self-trust that made each man his own authority on how to live.

Emerson's religious ideas were different than what he had been raised to believe. His forefathers had moved away from Calvinism toward Unitarianism. They retained a faith in man's absolute dependence on divine grace and on the religion that was revealed in the scriptures, although all-encompassing Unitarianism still carried the danger of spiritual presumptuousness. More than particular points of doctrine, religious service itself was a family tradition, and for five generations—starting with Joseph Emerson, who had been the minister of Mendon, Massachusetts in the mid-1600s—the family's clerical heritage had been fed by marriages with Blisses, Ripleys, Moodys and Bulkleys, all ministerial families themselves, so that Emerson and each of his four brothers were expected to make the sixth generation of ministers in the family line.

Emerson and his brothers did not receive the ministerial calling as a living tradition from their father, William Emerson: he died in 1811, when Emerson was eight. They did not receive it from their paternal grandfather, either: he had died in 1776, in the first winter of the Revolution, while serving as a chaplain to the Minutemen. Death was a frequent visitor to the Emerson family, and in addition to losing his father in 1811, Emerson lost an older brother in 1807, and two sisters, in infancy, in 1802 and 1814. Another brother, Robert Bulkley, was born mentally 'deficient': he would figure as a worry and a financial burden on the family until his death in 1836, but the Emerson family had a long tradition of faith to help them bear up under these losses and misfortunes.

Emerson and his brothers were groomed for the pulpit by their mother Ruth and her sister; by their step-grandfather, Ezra Ripley, and also by their father's younger sister, Mary Moody Emerson, a deeply religious spinster aunt who wore a funeral veil when she traveled, and was reputed to sleep in a coffin-shaped bed. In addition to telling the boys the stories that kept the family's religious heritage alive in their childhood poverty—for the loss of men had hurt the family's finances—Aunt Mary set the boys daunting challenges. She bade them not to speak unless they could speak truth, and to do, every day, what they were most afraid to do. Emerson described her in a sketch as

> Genius always new, subtle, frolicsome, musical, unpredictable. All your learning of all literatures & states of society, Platonistic, Calvinistic, English, or Chinese, would never enable you to anticipate one thought or expression …Nothing can excel the freedom & felicity of her letters,—such nobility is in this self rule, this absence of all reference to style or standard; it is the march of the mountain winds, the waving of flowers, or the flight of birds.

While Aunt Mary was a living link to the family's Calvinist past, she also set the boys an example by valuing her own experience of religious knowledge, and she would not accept scripture where experience would do. She wrote in her journal "Give me, my God, to know that it is thy immediate agency touches each nerve with pain, or digs the eye, or severs the bone. I can then, with thee, joy and praise for all the heights to which men and angels climb."

Waldo was Aunt Mary's favorite nephew, but as the second of the Emerson boys who survived to adulthood he was "accounted by the near relatives of the family as the least brilliant of the four." At age eighteen, he graduated from Harvard in the middle of his class, having accepted the position of class poet only after six of his classmates had turned it down. Emerson was somewhat restricted by the family's poverty: he spent in four years at Harvard about half of what wealthier students would spend in a year, and he worked through school as an errand boy for the college president. His older brother William's record was also middling, but William had borne the burden of putting Waldo through school. This labor was not wasted, though, and together, the two older brothers blazed a path for younger brothers Edward and Charles, each of whom graduated as the heads of their classes, each of whom delivered the valedictory orations at their commencements.

Regardless of his failure to distinguish himself, Emerson had come to Harvard at a propitious moment. Edward Everett had just been appointed to the Greek literature department, where he had reinvigorated the study of classical literature. Everett himself had only just returned from classical studies at Göttingen and then from his travels through Europe. With letters of introduction from Byron, he had traveled in Greece, where he had seen the landscapes of classical literature with his own eyes. Returning to Boston, he began to call for a literature that would express Americans' native experience as effectively as Homer had expressed the Greeks'. Everett's enthusiasm helped Waldo see literature and history as his own personal legacy, and Everett brought the classics so much to life that Emerson was not certain whether he ought to give up his divinity studies and try to be a writer instead.

The pressure to succeed their forefathers at the pulpit was a strong one, though, and each of his brothers evaded it. After graduating from Harvard, and then working as a teacher to put Waldo through school in turn, William had come back from his divinity studies in Germany full of doubts. He studied for the law instead of the church, and Edward and Charles both became lawyers after they finished at Harvard themselves. The family's ministerial history was nevertheless hard to turn away from, and each of the brothers suffered a crisis when they decided to take other paths. Only Emerson would commit himself to preaching, and only because he lacked the courage to try a writing career.

It was not only the rigors of divinity studies—or the need to live up to the family calling—that worried the Emerson brothers. They were all also haunted by the possibility that they might not be constitutionally strong enough to enter the clergy. Between their father's death in 1811, and the deaths of the brother and infant sisters, Emerson and his brothers were early accustomed to the loss or debility of family members, but they were none of them particularly healthy themselves, for all of the brothers suffered from tuberculosis, starting in their teens. Edward and Charles would die of it, in 1834 and 1836 respectively, and after he finished his divinity studies in 1826, Emerson himself would travel to South Carolina and Florida for his own health.

When Emerson returned to New England in 1827, at age twenty-four, he started to preach as a relief minister. He resisted any permanent position that would restrict his liberty, as he was still entertaining the possibility of a writing life. But on Christmas day, 1827, preaching in Concord, New Hampshire, he met and fell in love with Ellen Tucker, an aspiring poet of sixteen. Ellen was "very beautiful by universal consent...[and]

rich too," in his brother's account, and now that Emerson was returning to New Hampshire, to preach and to see Ellen again, he was starting to think about settling down to start a family of his own.

Waldo and Ellen were both the first among their siblings to fall in love. Love was completely new, and full of pleasant discoveries and surprises, powerful longings and miraculous sympathies. Six months into their engagement, Ellen wrote to him that—in contrast to her friend Elizabeth Sparhawk, who had rushed into a bad match—"we were *acquainted* Waldo only two weeks—and we seem so perfectly known to each other and (I will say) so perfectly satisfied with each other." Ellen's letters to Emerson are chatty, intimate and youthful. They are love-struck throughout, as Ellen frequently interrupted herself to exclaim, "I love you dearly Waldo." Emerson's letters to Ellen were lost: biographers speculate that he may have burned them after her death, unable to bear the spectre of his youthful, love-struck self. Visiting with the young couple, Waldo's brother William wrote to Charles: "these lovers are blind—purblind these lovers be."

Emerson's engagement was one of the high points of the late 1820s. His ordination in early 1828 as the Junior Minister of the prestigious Second Church of Boston, and his hasty promotion, in July 1828, to Head Minister, were others, but there was still sorrow to temper the excitement. Waldo and Ellen's courtship and marriage took place under the cloud of tuberculosis, which ran in the Tucker family as well in Emerson's. Ellen had lost a brother in 1825—and Ellen herself had already been coughing up blood by the time she met Emerson. She took her own illness with Calvinistic stoicism—she described "every pain [as] a scourge to the old sins that lurk within"—but she was still in such fragile health that Emerson wrote to his brother Charles in February 1828 that "she is too lovely to live long...Should she be struck out of existence tomorrow, it would still have been a rich blessing to have been permitted to have loved her."

In addition to Waldo's concern for Ellen, his brother Edward suffered a nervous breakdown in 1828, and had to be taken to an asylum. He recovered his mental health, but not without causing his family a great deal of worry, for he had always been regarded as the most brilliant of the brothers, and had been recruited to work in the law firm of Senator Daniel Webster, whose arguments before the Supreme Court had already earned him a prominent place in American politics. Having promised to bring the whole family distinction, Edward's breakdown was an affront to all of the Emerson brothers' possibilities. Between his brother's breakdown and Ellen's tuberculosis, then, Emerson's joys were well mixed with grief or apprehension, and the miracle of love must have seemed even more miraculous in contrast.

Tuberculosis notwithstanding, Waldo and Ellen were engaged in December 1828 and married in Concord, New Hampshire in September of 1829. Their deep personal love only seemed more divine for the threat of her death. Indeed, the flush of tuberculosis—and the glow of the nineteen-year-old's beauty—made it possible for Emerson to see Ellen as an angel, and her physical suffering made death seem not cruel but a benevolent and even merciful end to her pains. Ellen's seraphic appearance and her spiritual acceptance of her sufferings gave Emerson visions of a heavenly sphere where the lovers would be together forever, and in spite of all their diligent efforts—tragically, the prescribed long rides in the country and exercise probably only worsened her condition—Ellen died seventeen months after their marriage, at the beginning of February, 1831.

Emerson described his grief at her death as "sharpened into anguish by the 'complete wreck of earthly good.'" They had been so close that he was almost incapable of accepting that she was gone, and he kept her presence close as a living memory. Two hours after she died, he wrote to Aunt Mary, portraying the loss even as something of a relief:

> My angel is gone to heaven this morning & I am alone in the world & strangely happy...I have never known a person in the world in whose separate existence as a soul I could so readily & fully believe & she is present with me now beaming joyfully upon me, in her deliverance & the entireness of her love for [me]...Say, dear Aunt, if I am not rich in her memory?

Emerson continued to compose letters to Ellen as if she were still alive, and after fourteen months of making almost daily trips to her grave—in any kind of weather—he opened her casket: he wanted to see the decay for himself, and also to convince himself that she was gone (later in life he would open his son's casket as well, to see).

Holding on to Ellen's memory, Emerson grew impatient with the academic spirituality of the church. He wanted a living spirituality, not symbolic or received, but as present and palpable as his memory of Ellen—as close as the dead forefathers whom Aunt Mary had kept alive in him and in his brothers—as close as the brothers who "made but one man together." Emerson was still too alive to the spirit of his wife to take the daily lives of his parishioners—or even the institution of the church itself—very seriously, and less than a year after Ellen's death, he resigned his position, ostensibly over his unwillingness to offer the communion. He said that he had ceased to believe in the miracle of the rite, but the deeper reality was that the church and its forms could no longer sustain his faith. In Ellen's absence, he needed a personal, not an institutional consolation.

Emerson was partly compensated for his loss by an increase in liberty, as he inherited Ellen's portion of her father's estate—and then her sister's portion as well, when her sister died in 1833. This inheritance provided Emerson with two installments of $11,600,[1] the first of which, in 1834, gave him an

---

[1] Roughly $292,000 in 2012 dollars.

income of roughly $1,200 a year at interest[2] at a time when Emerson and his mother and Charles were renting a house for twelve dollars a week. This sum did not make Emerson rich—his family had never been wealthy, and there were debts to square in addition to the 'deficient' brother Bulkley to support in institutions—but it did allow him to help his brothers, and to support his mother—and he certainly benefited by having independence and free time in which to read and write, as well as freedom from the pressure of financial anxiety.

After resigning his pulpit, Emerson sailed for Europe on Christmas 1832, before the estate was even settled. Over the next year, he traveled from Malta to Britain, meeting with Landor and Wordsworth, Coleridge and Carlyle along the way. Emerson was inspired by his trip, which was marked by sublime experiences of nature. In the Jardin des Plants in Paris, where specimens were laid out by family and class, he had visions of the single spiritual unity that pervaded the universe and all of its various botanical, zoological and geologic forms. Coming home in 1833, he had a new confidence in a single living, animating spirit, and he would be known for this confidence forever after. Rather than slowly fading away, the spiritual connection Emerson had felt with Ellen's memory now filled the world as a living spirit that manifested itself in everything. The faith that sustained him through his loss—as well as the universalizing capacity, the powers of perception, concep-

---

[2] This had been his starting salary at the Second Church of Boston; it would be roughly $30,000 in 2012 dollars.

tion and reason he discovered in himself—compensated his loss by abstracting Ellen's living self into a living cosmos he could love as well as her. After this trip, Emerson would never feel deprived again. Even when Waldo, the first child of his second marriage, died in 1842, he mourned deeply, but he wrote in his essay "Experience" that

> In the death of my son, now more than two years ago, I seem to have lost a beautiful estate,—no more. I cannot get it nearer to me...this calamity...does not touch me: some thing which I fancied was a part of me, which could not be torn away without tearing me, nor enlarged without enriching me, falls off from me, and leaves no scar. It was caducous. I grieve that grief can teach me nothing, nor carry me one step into real nature.

In spite of all his losses—or perhaps even because of them—the loss of his father and siblings in childhood, and of Ellen in 1831—in addition, then, to the loss of his brothers Edward in 1834 and Charles in 1836—even in spite of Emerson's fears for his own health and mortality, his philosophy describes the universe as the outward manifestation of a divinity that resides in each man, as much as in all of the universe's forms, and it credits each and every man with the capacity to experience his own divine nature at first hand. "In the presence of nature," Emerson would write in *Nature* in 1836, "a wild delight runs through the man, in spite of real sorrows. Nature says,—he is my creature, and maugre all his impertinent griefs, he shall be glad with me."

THE DANGERS OF PASSION

On his return from Europe in 1833, then, Emerson started not only to write down his own spiritual experience, but also to declare America's creative, intellectual and spiritual independence. A mere fifty years after the Revolution, America was still a derivative country, without a culture of its own, but Emerson used his confidence in the single living divinity he had seen, which pervaded all of nature's forms, to urge Americans to look to their own surroundings, and to disregard the authority of received religions and institutions. As he wrote in the preface to *Nature* in 1836,

> The foregoing generations beheld God and nature face to face; we, through their eyes. Why should not we also enjoy an original relation to the universe? Why should not we have a poetry and philosophy of insight and not of tradition, and a religion by revelation to us, and not the history of theirs?... The sun shines to-day also. There is more wool and flax in the fields. There are new lands, new men, new thoughts. Let us demand our own works and laws and worship.

Emerson's visions developed along with a quintessentially democratic rhetorical stance, for he wrote and he spoke in an oracular voice, and even when he spoke for himself, he was disavowing his particular self—he was only speaking for the best man each is to himself.

Emerson had continued to preach while he was writing, but mainly he was developing his ideas in a series of public lectures he gave in Lyceums. Lyceums were lecture halls where visiting speakers addressed topics ranging from self-cultivation and etiquette to political themes such as abolition or women's rights, and Emerson used his lectures, beginning with a series on the "Uses of Natural History," as a testing ground for the ideas that would coalesce in his essays. In the secular setting of the Lyceum, his oracular tone and his talk of self-reliance earned him receptive audiences among the middle class of a young nation apprehensive about the vitality and originality of its culture.

In 1835—while Fuller, at twenty-five, was agonizing over the possibility of ever finding an intellectual guide—Emerson married again at thirty-two. Preaching in Portsmouth, New Hampshire in 1834, he had met Lydia Jackson, who was, as one of Emerson's friends later described her, a

> singular looking person, and to my thinking, very handsome. Her eyes are somewhat like lamps, and the expression of her face is that of a beaming soul, shining through. Then, when she talks, she thinks; and you see it. Her movements are free and graceful; she is a soaring transcendentalist; she is full of sensibility, yet as independent in her mind as—who shall I say? Margaret Fuller.

Lydia was a year older than Emerson. At thirty-three, she was still unmarried, as she had been taking care of the family household. Emerson was taken by her at once. Their daughter Ellen later wrote that "what Father admired in her was 'her air of lofty abstraction, like Dante,'" and Lydia's abstraction was the outward appearance of a religious nature similar to Emerson's. Ellen wrote that a friend of Lydia's, after hearing Emerson preach, told her that "what Mr Emerson said was just what you always say."

When Emerson described Lydia in a journal entry, he was passive in his own love:

> There are some occult facts in human nature that are natural magic. The chief of these is the glance…The mysterious communication that is established across a house between two entire strangers, by this means, moves all the springs of wonder. It happened once that a youth & a maid beheld each other in a public assembly for the first time. The youth gazed with great delight upon the beautiful face until he caught the maiden's eye. She presently became aware of his attention & something like correspondence immediately takes place. The maid depressed her eyes that the man might gaze upon her face. Then the man looked away, that the maiden might gratify her curiosity. Presently their eyes met in a full, front, searching, not to be mistaken glance. It is wonderful how much it made them acquainted. The man thought that they had come nearer together than they could by any other intercourse in months.

In January 1835, Emerson wrote to propose marriage, in a proposal that is most notable for its impersonality:

The strict limits of the intercourse I have enjoyed, have certainly not permitted the manifestation of that tenderness which is the first sentiment in the common kindness between man and woman. But I am not less in love, after a new and higher way. I have immense desire that you should love me, and that I might live with you always. My own assurance of the truth and fitness of the alliance—the union I desire, is so perfect, that it will not admit the thought of hesitation—never of refusal on your part. I would scratch out the word. I am persuaded that I address one so in love with what I love, so conscious with me of the everlasting principles, and seeking the presence of the common Father through means so like, that no remoteness of condition could much separate us, and that an affection founded on such a basis, cannot falter.

I will not embarrass this expression of my heart and mind with any second considerations. I am not therefore blind to them. They touch the past and the future—our friends as well as ourselves, & even the Departed. But I see clearly how your consent shall resolve them all.

Lydia had not anticipated the proposal. According to Ellen's biography, she

was utterly amazed. How could he condescend to her? And then how little he knew her!...She asked Father [Emerson] to come and talk with her on the subject. He came at once, of course. She...told him that she foresaw that with her long life wholly aside from housekeeping she should not be a skillful mistress of a house and that it would be a load of care and labour from which she shrank and a giving up of an existence she thoroughly enjoyed and to which she had become exactly fitted, and she could not undertake it unless he was sure he loved her and needed her enough to justify her in doing it, and many questions she asked him.... It was settled that day.

The marriage proposal may have been settled, but the passion they shared seems to have remained predominantly spiritual. As soon as their relationship began, Emerson renamed Lydia 'Lidian'—ostensibly to avoid the harsh inevitable Boston pronunciation "Lidiar"—but also to etherealize her, to turn her into an angel, for his first use of the name is as a term of exaltation. Nor could Lidian, for her part, relinquish a certain formality, but Ellen wrote that "she could not call Father anything but Mr Emerson, which he did not like. He had asked her several times to call him Waldo, but she could not." Ellen also remarked that "the tremendous manner in which she loved Father was always as astonishing to me as the coolness with which she treated him" and Emerson himself wrote that he took a "very sober joy" in his second wife.

When Emerson married Lidian in September 1835, he had already been deeply in love, he had already been married, and now he was building his career on the visions he had seen, in his love of Ellen, and then in the world that preserved her presence after she died. This marriage was not a passionate tie. Lidian bore him four children—something Ellen had not been able to do—and now that she was devoted to the business of raising a family and running the household, she could compete neither with his memory of Ellen nor with his literary-spiritual work. During the first trimester of her pregnancy, Emerson wrote in his journal,

> In life all finding is not the thing we sought, but something else. The lover on being accepted, misses the wildest charm of the maid he dared not hope to call his own. The husband loses the wife in the cares of the household. Later, he cannot rejoice with her in the babe for by becoming a mother she ceases yet more to be a wife.

Their first son, Waldo, was born at the end of October 1836, shortly after *Nature* was published in September. A daughter was born in 1839, and when Lidian suggested that they name the girl Ellen, he wrote in his journal that "Lidian…magnanimously makes my gods her gods."

IV

EMERSON HAD ALWAYS SHARED HIS HOUSE WITH HIS FAMILY, and after his wedding in New Hampshire, he brought Lidian to the house he had recently bought in Concord, Massachusetts. There the couple lived with Emerson's mother Ruth, and with his brother Charles, starting in September 1835. Charles' fiancée, Elizabeth Hoar, became so close to Waldo, and also to Lidian, that even after Charles died in May 1836, Emerson and his wife invited her to live with them, since they were more likely to understand her than her own family was.

After his controversial Divinity School Address in 1838, Emerson was beginning to be known widely for his views, as he was urging people to know their own religious experience, and to make their own religious decisions. In spite of the disapproval of Harvard sages, he was beginning to draw people toward his ideas, and Ellen wrote of the late 1830s,

> Now began what Mother called Transcendental Times. Either now or earlier Father gave up family prayers. Mother and Grandmother mourned together, and together read the Bible and a hymn for a long time...Mother had always felt as if Father's & her religious views were the same...Now it was clear to her that he was not a Christian in her sense of the word, and it was a most bitter discovery.

If Lidian regretted Emerson's self-reliant spirituality, there were plenty of intellectuals and aspiring poets and writers who sought him out for his ideas, and now that Emerson was married and settled in Concord, he began to expand his circle by inviting visitors to the house. The Emersons were, as Ellen said, "hospitably disposed," and guests came so regularly that their cook threatened to "put a poster out at the gate 'This House is not a Hotel.'" It was during this time that Emerson hosted Harriet Martineau and then Fuller.

Emerson was throwing open his doors to others as well: in September 1836, shortly after Fuller's visit, and shortly after *Nature* was published, he founded the Transcendental Club as a forum for encouraging a new vitality in American ideas. One of the other founders was Henry Hedge, who had been a precocious student like Fuller—by age seven, Hedge had Vergil's *Eclogues* by heart and, by ten, "whole books of Homer's *Iliad*." Hedge had left Boston to study in Germany a few years after Edward Everett, and he shared Everett's passion for German literature and Goethe with Fuller. The Transcendental Club moved from one house to another for meetings every two or three months over the next four years, promoting the discussion of topics such as 'American Genius,' 'Mysticism and Christianity' or 'the Nature of Poetry and Poets.' Many of the Club members—Bronson Alcott, Orestes Brownson, or Henry David Thoreau among them—were already prominent writers, reformers, preachers or artists, and many of the more than thirty others were on the verge of launching prominent careers. Lidian was included in this circle, but the intellectual passion for innovation and self-reliance was not on her side. She responded tartly to the new talk of what its detractors were calling Transcendentalism, and she wrote a "Transcendental Bible," which caricatured her husband's optimism: "Never speak of sin," she wrote. "It is of no consequence to 'the Being' whether *you* are good or bad. It is egotistical to consider it yourself; who are you?"

V

FOR ALL OF THE GENERAL FERMENT OF IDEAS, Fuller's appearance at Emerson's house still marked the beginning of an era in Emerson's life. Her rigorous education had prepared her particularly well for Emerson's brand of self-reliance, for her education and her experience had made her an independent thinker, with a broad expanse of literature at her command. But she was also personally interested in Emerson, as a possible mentor and guide, and her personal interest stimulated him in turn, moving him to write that "of personal influence, speaking strictly,—an efflux, that is, purely of mind and character...she had an extraordinary degree; I think more than any person I have known. An interview with her was a joyful event." After two weeks of knowing Fuller, Emerson added in his journal, "She is quite an extraordinary person for her apprehensiveness her acquisitions & her powers of conversation. It is always a great refreshment to see a very intelligent person. It is like being set in a large place. You stretch your limbs & dilate to your utmost size." In the *Memoirs*, he would describe Fuller's arrival as

> a holiday, and so was her abode. She stayed a few days, often a week, more seldom a month, and all tasks that could be suspended were put aside to catch the favorable hour, in

walking, riding, or boating, to talk with this joyful guest, who brought wit, anecdotes, love-stories, tragedies, oracles with her, and, with her broad web of relations to so many fine friends, seemed like the queen of some parliament of love, who carried the key to all confidences.

Meeting Emerson marked a profound shift for Fuller as well: here was a man whose knowledge might hold hers to account. Recollecting their friendship years later, she wrote:

> Emerson's influence has been more beneficial to me than that of any other American... from him I first learned what is meant by an inward life...That the "mind is its own place," was a dead phrase to me, till he cast light upon my mind...It would take a volume to tell what this one influence did for me.

In addition to exchanging visits, friendship for Emerson and Fuller consisted of a rapid exchange of ideas, books and intimacies. Emerson wrote, "I believe I had the pleasure of making her acquainted with Chaucer, with Ben Jonson, with Herbert, Chapman, Ford, Beaumont and Fletcher, with Bacon, and Sir Thomas Browne." For her part, Fuller introduced Emerson to Goethe and German literature, particularly Eckermann's *Conversations with Goethe* and Bettine von Arnim's *Goethe's Conversations with a Child*, and this latter volume would color their own friendship with the complex interplay of Goethe's authority and the younger von Arnim's passionate admiration.

For Fuller, at least, marriage was always in the background of this exchange. Goethe had inspired her to think of herself as being outside of marriage, and when she was translating Goethe in the late 1830s, she would write in her journal,

> I think it perfectly true (though in no gross or sneering sense) what Goethe [says] that women who love and marry feel no need to write. But how can a woman of genius love and marry? A man of genius will not love her; he wants repose. She may find some object sufficient to excite her ideal for a time but love perishes as soon as it finds it has grasped the shadow for substance. Divorce must take place for the large nature will not find one capable of continuing its consort. Nor can children of the flesh satisfy the longing of the spirit for its maternity…Such a woman cannot long remain wed, again she is single, again must seek and strive. Social wedlock is ordinarily mere subterfuge and simulacrum: it could not check a powerful woman or a powerful man.

As Emerson and Fuller's friendship deepened, their correspondence seemed to promise a transcendental intimacy beyond marriage. When Emerson wrote to Fuller about von Arnim's book, there was nothing to prevent her from taking his letter as an implicit prophecy of their own friendship:

> It seems to me she [von Arnim] is the only formidable test that was applied to Goethe's genius. He could well abide any other influence under which he came. Here was genius purer than his own…and…[Goethe] does not make one

THE DANGERS OF PASSION

adequate confession of the transcendent superiority of this woman's aims and affections in the presence of which all his Art must have struck sail.

Nor was Emerson sparing in encouraging Fuller in her work. In June, 1838, he wrote to Fuller to express his indebtedness after having read from a manuscript of her journals, letters and poems:

I found no dulness in it but very sprightly sense & criticism & brave determination, & truth throughout...I perceive that I owe several *things* to the book quite new to me & as a history of fine things, I prize it very highly. Can I see it again? & again as it grows? So shall I have presence in two places.

In May, 1839, picking up one of their conversations, he wrote,

I know that not possibly can you write a bad book a dull page, if you only indulge yourself and take up your work somewhat proudly, if the same friend bestows her thoughts on Goethe who plays now at the game of conversation & now writes a journal rich gay perceptive & never dull.

Emerson was not always writing as an elder and mentor, though: he also took the tone of an aspirant himself: "I do not think I shall be a whit behind yourself in my admiration of any noble gift though I may be slower in discovering it." Emerson and Fuller were so well suited to each other that Elizabeth Hoar wrote that Fuller's "power of bringing out Mr. Emerson has doubled my enjoyment of that blessing to be in one house and room with him."

Fuller's effect on Emerson was measured not only in her presence but in her friends as well, several of whom had become close friends of Emerson's. Emerson wrote in the *Memoirs* that "a life of Margaret is impossible without [her friends]." They were, he said, "a fair, commanding troop, every one of them adorned by some splendor of beauty, of grace, of talent, or of character, and comprising in their band persons who have since disclosed sterling worth and elevated aims in the conduct of life." After "a sincerely good visit from Caroline Sturgis," he wrote to Fuller in June 1839: "Shall you introduce me to your Recamier[3] this summer? So am I always your debtor." Having finally met Anna Barker, he wrote to thank Fuller: "I would not on any account have failed to see Anna Barker that very human piece of divinity in whom grace goodness & wit have so constitutional a blending that she quite defies all taking to pieces." Fuller also introduced Emerson to Sam Ward, who had by now returned from Europe, and by 1839, Emerson, Fuller, Ward, Barker and Sturgis were trading letters and visits with open intimacy.

Fuller herself benefited materially when Emerson introduced her to Bronson Alcott, the Transcendentalist writer and

---

[3] Anna Barker, whom Fuller had earlier compared to Madame Récamier (b. 1830) the salonniere who was Madame de Staël's companion for a time. Emerson's comparison puts Fuller in the role of Madame de Staël.

teacher. Alcott was opening a progressive school in Boston in 1836, and Fuller taught at his school for a year before he closed it. In 1837 she taught in his disciple Hiram Fuller's[4] school in Providence, Rhode Island, where she proved to be immensely popular with her students. Emerson recalled a "lady who knew her well" saying that "had she been a man, any one of those fine girls of sixteen, who surrounded her here, would have married her: they were all in love with her, she understood them so well." The letters Emerson and Fuller exchanged in this period were full of literary criticism and evaluations, in addition to observations of nature, human nature, morality and society, and by 1838, many of Emerson's longest letters were to Fuller—by early 1840 some of the most rhapsodic as well.

Fuller quit teaching in 1839, because it demanded too much energy from her, and it was keeping her from her writing. She moved to Boston with her mother and started a Conversations course for women. For a fee of $20[5] each, between twenty and forty women discussed the problems of the day from literary, intellectual, spiritual and feminist perspectives; men were invited rarely, typically with a chilling effect on conversation. Fuller started with Greek mythology, but conversations circled around a fundamental question: "what were we born to do: and how shall we do it?" From November 1839 through the spring of 1844, this discussion series provided Fuller with a steady income, in addition to a widening circle of friends and

[4] No relation.
[5] Roughly $500 in 2012 dollars.

an acknowledged intellectual authority. Now she could write to and visit with Emerson more freely, as she was deriving her income—like him—solely from her own intellectual labors.

Shared interests involved Emerson and Fuller in projects that continued to bring them closer and closer. By 1839, the Transcendentalists planned to publish a literary journal—"not to multiply books, but to report life"—and Fuller took the first turn as the editor of *The Dial*. The journal occasioned a great deal of correspondence between Emerson and Fuller, and their letters assumed a jocular, familiar tone. By the end of 1839, Emerson was still making veiled promises in his letters, and Fuller could still feel that she was making inroads into his personality. "You are as good—it may be better than ever—to your poor hermit," he wrote her. "He will come yet to know the world through your eyes." If that were not encouraging enough, he closed his letter by confessing that her letters and poem, as well as a clipping from her journals had made him

> a little impatient of my honourable prison—my quarantine of temperament wherefrom I deal courteously with all comers, but through cold water...I should like once in my life to be pommelled black & blue with sincere words...
>
> I joy in your studies & success. Continue to befriend me....
>
> Ward has given me [a print of] Endymion! I delight much in what I dreamed not of in my first acquaintance with you—my new relations to your friends.

If Emerson was practically asking Fuller to pommel him, it was because he had never seen himself as a social person. As a minister, he had been dismissed from the deathbed of one of his parishioners because he could not think of anything to say to the dying man. He confessed to his journal in November, 1839 that "most of the persons whom I see in my own house I see across a gulf. I cannot go to them nor they come to me. Nothing can exceed the frigidity & labor of my speech with such...I see the ludicrousness of the plight as well as they." Friendship with Fuller was finally challenging his sense of his own reclusiveness, though, and Emerson may have been writing to himself as well, when he proposed to Fuller that "we will be equal to an Idea so divine as Friendship." There were moments when he seemed glad to be pulled out of himself: in response to a packet of reading Fuller had sent, he wrote in December of 1839,

> I...startled my mother & my wife when I went into the dining room with the declaration that I wished to live a little while with people who love & hate, who have Muses & Furies, and in a twelvemonth I should write tragedies & romance...You are brave, and in your relation to your friends shall be always honoured and long hereafter thanked.

The power Fuller had, to elevate another person by her presence, was an unspoken power at the heart of Transcendentalism, but it was always impossible to account for, because

Transcendentalism was centered on the individual's experience of divinity in nature. In spite of their Club meetings and their plans for a literary journal, the Transcendentalists still professed that other people were not supposed to mediate or influence the self in its discoveries, and they were careful to avoid the appearance of dependency of one upon another. Transcendental friendship was not supposed to lead to marriage—it was supposed to elevate friends' intercourse above love. The highest goal was self-reliance, where individuals could meet as equals, beyond the unequal relations in marriage, which was still a domestic, economic relationship, more than a form of shared personal or spiritual life.

Fuller expected a great deal of intimacy from her friendships, and she was already used to seeing her friends as spiritual entities. In 1842, she recalled the sublimity of her friendship with Anna Barker, whom she had met in 1830, when they were both twenty:

> It is so true that a woman may be in love with a woman, and a man with a man. It is so pleasant to be sure of it because undoubtedly it is the same love we shall feel when we are angels when we ascend to the only fit place for Mignons, where *Sie fragen nicht nach Mann und Weib*.[6]—It is regulated by the same love as that of love between persons of different sexes, only it is purely intellectual and spiritual, unprofaned by any mixture of lower instincts. ...Thus the beautiful seeks the strong, and the strong the

---

[6] "It is not a question of man or woman." Bell Gale Chevigny's translation.

> beautiful…I loved Anna for a time with as much passion as I was then strong enough to feel.

This spiritualizing language could not be reconciled with personal affections, though—it had only obscured Fuller's feelings for her friend Sam Ward, whom she had met through Liza Farrar in 1835. They had become close friends, and while engagement was never explicitly assumed, their spiritualized friendship and their shared passions for literature and art had allowed Fuller to assume that they belonged to each other. When Ward withdrew from her in 1839, she could not say that she loved him, exactly, when she wrote to express her disappointment:

> We were truly friends, but it was not friends as men are friends to one another, or as brother and sister. There was, also, that pleasure, which may, perhaps, be termed conjugal, of finding oneself in an alien nature…
>
> I think I may say, I never loved…As in a glass darkly, I have seen what I might feel as child, wife, mother, but I have never really approached the close relations of life. A sister I have been to many—a brother to more—a fostering nurse to, oh how many! The bridal hour of many a spirit, when first it was wed, I have shared, but said adieu before the wine was poured out at the banquet.

This aspiration to non-matrimonial intimacy, which was patterned after von Arnim's letters to Goethe, colored all of the Transcendentalists' correspondence, so that Caroline Sturgis was not considered too forward when she wrote to Emerson, in 1839, "I know I have never been anything but a child, but perhaps I shall sometime learn to be a woman. I wish to have the actual thing as it stands, neither more nor less, will you not give it to me as far as you can, and not throw tint and clouds into the shining sky?"

Emerson corresponded with Fuller and Sturgis and Barker and Ward alike in these terms, but this degree of elevation and openness did not come easily for him. He was older than Fuller by seven years—he was sixteen years older than Sturgis—and while he benefited by his friends' enthusiasm—and while his learning gave their ideas a far-reaching resonance—his habits and his reputation were more formed than theirs. However much he might have "wished to live a little while with people who love & hate," he already had a wife—and, by 1839, two infant children—so he did not feel the same pressure Fuller and Sturgis felt, to turn his friends into mentors and guides.

For the first years of their friendship, this difference had been comprehended by the jocular tone Emerson assumed when he described himself as Fuller's 'poor hermit'—but this changed when Sam Ward and Anna Barker announced their engagement in the summer of 1840. It had been less than a year since Fuller had lost Ward's affections, but Ward and Barker's engagement was a disappointment for Emerson, Fuller and Sturgis alike, and each of them felt the engagement as a loss or a betrayal. When Ward had withdrawn from Fuller in 1839, she had lost more than a friend: she lost the possibility that Ward might indeed become the one who could 'comprehend her wholly, mentally and morally, and enable her to better comprehend herself.' But Emerson and Sturgis felt excluded by their engagement as well: Emerson himself had elevated Ward—referring to him as 'Raphael' in his letters to Barker, Ward and Fuller—and now he wrote to Sturgis that

> I thought [Barker] had looked the world through for a man as universal as herself and finding none, had said, "I will compensate myself for my great renunciation as a woman by establishing ideal relations; not only Raphael shall be my brother, but that Puritan at Concord…I will elect him also."

As Fuller, Emerson and Sturgis each probed their sense of disappointment—as they started to clarify what they needed and what they wanted from each other—the differences in their expectations erupted into open disagreement. Emerson did not make any claims on Barker's affections—he just struggled to master his own disappointment—but for Fuller, the disappointment of being excluded this time was painful. She could not make claims on Ward or on Barker, but in her friendship with Emerson, she saw a power that might compensate her loss. She wrote in her journal:

> I am bent on being his only friend myself. There is enough of me would I but reveal it. Enough of woman to sympa-

thize with all his feelings, enough of man to appreciate all thoughts. I could be a perfect friend and it would make me a nobler person. I would never indulge towards him that need of devotion which lies at the depth of my being. He measures too much, he is too reasonable. I could not be my truest childlike self. But I might be my truest manlike self.

Sturgis shared Fuller's disappointment, and in August of 1840, they pressed Emerson, in person, for a greater intimacy. Emerson resisted them; he wrote in his journal, "[Margaret] and C[aroline]. would gladly be my friends, yet our intercourse is not friendship, but literary gossip."

Sensing Emerson's resistance, Fuller and Sturgis accused him of aloofness, and now when Emerson wrote to Sturgis, he was more even reticent about the possibilities in their friendship:

I dare not engage my peace so far as to make you necessary to me as I can easily see any establishment of habitual intercourse would do, when the first news I may hear is that you have found in some heaven foreign to me your mate, & my beautiful castle is exploded to shivers. Then I take the other part & say, Shall I not trust this chosen child that not possibly will she deceive a noble expectation or content herself with less than greatness[.] When she gives herself away it will be only to an equal virtue, then will I gain a new friend without utter loss of that which now is. But that which set me on this writing was the talk with Margaret F last Friday who taxed me on both your parts with a certain inhospitality of soul inasmuch as you were both willing to be my friends in the full & sacred sense & I remained apart critical, & after many interviews still a stranger. I count & weigh, but do not love.—I heard the charge, I own, with great humility and sadness. I confess to the fact of cold & imperfect discourse, but not to the impeachment of my will. [sic] and not to the deficiency of my affection. If I count & weigh, I love also. I cannot tell you how warm & glad the naming of your names makes my solitude. You give me more joy than I could trust my tongue to tell you. Perhaps it is ungrateful never to testify by word to those whom we love, how much they are our benefactors. But to my thought this is better to remain a secret from the lips to soften only the behavior.

But I do not get nearer to you. Whose fault is that? With all my heart I would live in your society I would gladly spend the remainder of my days in the holy society of the best the wisest & the most beautiful[.] Come & live near me whenever it suits your pleasure & if you will confide in me so far I will engage to be as true a brother to you as ever blood made. But I thank you for saying that you were sure of me, in reply to M.s wish. The ejaculation and the reply were both delicious to me.

This letter did not make an end to the crisis, though. In his next letter to Sturgis, his tone was more resigned:

I hate everything frugal and cowardly in friendship. *That*, at least should be brave and generous. When we fear the

> withdrawal of love from ourselves by the new relations which our companions must form, it is mere infidelity. We believe in our eyes and not in the Creator...So, dear child, I give you up to all your Gods—to your wildest love and pursuit of beauty, to the boldest effort of your Imagination to express it, to the most original choices of tasks and influences and the rashest exclusion of all you deem alien or malign;—and you shall not give me so great joy as by the finding for yourself a love which shall make mine show cold and feeble—which certainly is not cold or feeble.

It is not exactly clear what Sturgis and Fuller demanded of Emerson, as the original complaints were lodged in person. Surely they were not asking for extra-marital intimacies, but after Ward and Barker's engagement, it seems clear they could not continue to be satisfied with literary transcendentalism and epistolary passion. Judging by Emerson's defensive responses, he may have felt as if Fuller and Sturgis were asking him to confess an intimacy too close to personal love. Perhaps he felt that Fuller was essentially asking him to express a longing for a deeper relationship between them, even in spite of—and even perhaps *because* of—the fact that such a deep relationship would be impossible. If Emerson felt that Fuller was asking him to wish, with her, for an impossible relationship, she may have been touching his grief for Ellen, or his brothers—the other impossible relationships he had managed to sustain by elevating longing into writing.

Whatever the cause, Emerson could not confess himself to Fuller—or to Sturgis. In September, he elaborated his defense in his journal:

> You would have me love you. What shall I love? Your body? The supposition disgusts you. What you have thought & said? Well, whilst you were thinking and saying them, but not now. I see no possibility of loving any thing but what now is, & is becoming; your courage, your enterprize, your budding affection, your opening thought, your prayer I can love,—but what else.

As the conversation continued to simmer through August and September and even to the end of October of 1840, Emerson's responses grew more measured, diplomatic and aloof, relinquishing his friends to the world. He wrote to Fuller in September:

> Since I have been an exile so long from the social world and a social world is now thrust upon me...I will study to deserve my friends—I abandon myself to what is best in you all...We are likely, my dear friend, soon to prove among us whether more than two can speak together.

To Caroline Sturgis, he wrote, "I will identify you with the Ideal Friend, & live with you on imperial terms. Present, you shall be present only as an angel might be, & absent you shall not be absent from me. So let these tides of the Infinite...roll unchecked for me, for thee, their everlasting circles."

Fuller refused to be spiritualized, though—she appears to have continued enumerating their differences instead. Again Emerson responded defensively:

> In your last letter...you...do say...that I am yours & yours shall be, let me dally how long soever in this or that other temporary relation. I on the contrary do constantly aver that you and I are not inhabitants of one thought of the Divine Mind, but of two thoughts, that we meet and treat like foreign states, one maritime, one inland, whose trade and laws are essentially unlike. I find or fancy in your theory a certain willfulness and not pure acquiescence which seems to me the only authentic mode. Our friend is part of our fate; those who dwell in the same truth are friends; those who are exercised on different thoughts are not, & must puzzle each other for the time...I am willing to see how unskilfully I make out a case of difference & will open all my doors to your sunshine & morning air.

Not to be dismissed with abstractions, Fuller continued to press for personal recognition. She quoted Emerson's words back to him, reproaching him for failing to fulfill his philosophy at the same time that she defended herself against his charge of presuming too much.

> I have felt the impossibility of meeting far more than you; so much, that if you ever know me well, you will feel that the fact of my abiding by you thus far, affords a strong proof that we are to be much to one another. How often have I left you despairing and forlorn. How often have I

said, this light will never understand my fire; this clear eye will never discern the law by which I am filling my circle; this simple force will never interpret my need for manifold being.

Dear friend on one point misinterpret me less. I do not love power other than every vigorous nature delights to feel itself living. To violate the sanctity of relations, I am as far from it as you can be. I make no claim. I have no wish which is not dictated by a feeling of truth. Could I lead the highest Angel captive by a look, that look I would not give, unless prompted by true love. I am no usurper. I ask only mine own inheritance. If it be found that I have mistaken its boundaries, I will give up the choicest vineyard, the fairest flower garden, to its lawful owner…[sic]

In me I did not think you saw the purity, the singleness, into which, I have faith that all this darting motion, and restless flame shall yet be attempered and subdued. I felt that you did not for me the highest office of friendship, by offering me the clue to the labyrinth of my own being. Yet I thought you appreciated the fearlessness which shrinks from no truth in myself & others, & trusted me, believing that I knew the path for myself. O it must be that you have felt the worth of that truth which has never hesitated to infringe on our relation, or aught else, rather than not vindicate itself…when my soul, in its childish agony of prayer, stretched out its arms to you as a father, did you not see what was meant by this crying for the moon; this sullen rejection of playthings which had become unmeaning? Did you then say, "I know not what this means; perhaps this will trouble me; the time will come when I shall hide my eyes from this mood;"—then you are not the friend I seek.

But did you not ask for a "foe" in your friend? Did you not ask for a "large formidable nature"? But a beautiful foe, I am not yet, to you. Shall I ever be? I know not. My life is now prayer…

But oh, I am now full of such sweet certainty, never never more can it be shaken. All things have I given up to the central power, myself, you also; yet, I cannot forbear adding, dear friend. I am now so at home, I know not how again to wander and grope, seeking my place in another soul. I need to be recognized. After this I shall be claimed, rather than claim, yet if I speak of facts, it must be as I see them.

As the dispute persisted, it began to resonate beyond their friendship, and soon Emerson was justifying the aloofness in his writing in the same terms as he had been defending himself against Fuller's accusations:

When I write a letter to any one whom I love, I have no lack of words or thoughts: I am wiser than myself & read my paper with the pleasure of one who receives a letter, but what I write to full up the gaps of a chapter is hard & cold, is grammar & logic; there is no magic in it; I do not wish to see it again. Settle with yourself your accusations of me. If I do not please you, ask me not to please you, but please yourself. What you call my indolence nature does not accuse.

THE DANGERS OF PASSION

Fuller had yet to settle her accusations—nor could she abandon what she saw as her obligation, as Emerson's friend. Later that same month, she wrote to Sturgis,

> Waldo is still only a small and secluded part of Nature, secluded by a doubt, secluded by a sneer. I am ashamed of him for the letter he wrote about our meeting.—It is equally unworthy of him and of what he professes for you. He calls you his sister and his saint yet he cannot trust your sight. There are many beings who have reached a height of generosity and freedom far above him.
>
> But none is truer, purer, and he is already profound....
>
> I cannot read these letters without a great renewal of my desire to teach this sage all he wants to make him the full-formed Angel. But that task is not for me. The gulf which separates us is too wide.

Finally Emerson began to concede the discussion, and to abandon ground he could not defend. He wrote to Fuller on October 20, "A strong passion or a fit work...the first will never come to such as I am; the second I do not absolutely despair of." Backing away from any explicit dependence upon friends, he ended the argument in a letter on October 24.

> I ought never to have suffered you to lead me into any conversation or writing on our relation, a topic from which with all persons my Genius ever sternly warns me away. I was content & happy to meet on a human footing a woman of sense & sentiment with whom one could ex-

change reasonable words & go away assured that wherever she went there was light & force & honour. That is to me a solid good; it gives value to thought & the day; it redeems society from that foggy & misty aspect it wears so often seen from our retirements; it is the foundation of everlasting friendship. Touch it not—speak not of it—and this most welcome natural alliance becomes from month to month,—& the slower & with the more intervals the better,—our air & diet...But tell me that I am cold or unkind, and in my most flowing state I become a cake of ice. I can feel the crystals shoot & the drops solidify. It may do for others but it is not for me to bring the relation to speech. Instantly I find myself a solitary unrelated person, destitute not only of all social faculty but of all private substance...

There is a difference in our constitution. We use a different rhetoric. It seems as if we had been born & bred in different nations. You say you understand me wholly. You cannot communicate yourself to me. I hear the words sometimes but remain a stranger to your state of mind[.]

Yet are we all the time a little nearer. I honor you for a brave & beneficent woman and mark with gladness your steadfast good will to me. I see not how we can bear each other anything else than good will...

And now what will you? Why should you interfere? See you not that I cannot spare you? that you cannot be spared? that a vast & beautiful Power to whose counsels our will was never party, has thrown us into strict neighborhood for best & happiest ends? The stars in Orion do not quarrel this night, but shine in peace in their old society. Are we not much better than they? Let us live as we have always done. only [sic] ever better, I hope, & richer. Speak to me of every thing but myself & I will endeavor to make an intelligible reply. Allow me to serve you & you will do me a kindness; come & see me & you will recommend my house to me; let me visit you and I shall be cheered as ever by the spectacle of so much genius & character as you have always the gift to draw around you.

I see very dimly in writing on this topic. It will not prosper with me. Perhaps my words are all wrong. Do not expect it of me again for a very long time.

This was the last word—Fuller did not press him any further.

VI

NINE MONTHS LATER, IN JULY 1841, the dispute was far enough in the past that Emerson could refer to it flatly in a letter to Fuller: "They say in heaven that I am a very awkward lover of my friends," he wrote. "Granted...—but a sincere one. My love reacts on me like the recoiling gun. It is pain." Continuing, he offered the explanation that "the cause of that barrier some time talked of between us two, is that I have no barrier, but am all boundless conceding & willowy." By November 1841, he was writing to Fuller with diplomatic formality: "I say to myself, it is surely very generous in such a rich & great minded woman to throw her steady light on me also, and to love me so well. I think better of the whole Universe, and resolve never to be mean. So now do not withdraw your rays: but still forgive all my incapacities; and it shall be counted to you for righteousness with all angels."

Not having attained the intimacy she sought, Fuller withdrew to seek mentors and guides elsewhere, and others beside Fuller charged Emerson with inhospitality of soul. Throughout the autumn of 1840, while Emerson had been besieged by Fuller and Sturgis, Emerson's friend George Ripley had been trying to convince him to sell his house in Concord, and to join the new utopian community at Brook Farm. Already on the defensive, Emerson declined, but he must have been touching raw nerves when he wrote to Ripley in December that "I do not look on myself as a valuable member to any community which is not either very large or very small & select...Moreover I am so ignorant & uncertain in my improvements that I would fain hide my attempts & failures in solitude."

Emerson was still not finished answering Fuller's complaints about his coldness. He was meditating on individuality and society in the essays he wrote over the winter of 1840-1841. In "Self-Reliance," he defended his need for solitude, even as he promised the same transcendence—the same possibility of a truer, newer relation between truth seekers—that had drawn Fuller to him in the first place:

> Live no longer to the expectation of these deceived and deceiving people with whom we converse. Say to them, 'O father, O mother, O wife, O brother, O friend, I have lived with you after appearances hitherto. Henceforward I am the truth's. Be it known unto you that henceforward I obey no law less than the eternal law. I will have no covenants but proximities. I shall endeavour to nourish my parents, to support my family, to be the chaste husband of one wife,—but these relations I must fill after a new and unprecedented way. I appeal from your customs. I must be myself. I cannot break myself any longer for you, or you. If you can love me for what I am, we shall be the happier. If you cannot, I will still seek to deserve that you should. I will not hide my tastes or aversions. I will so trust that

what is deep is holy, that I will do strongly before the sun and moon whatever inly rejoices me, and the heart appoints. If you are noble, I will love you; if you are not, I will not hurt you and myself by hypocritical attentions. If you are true, but not in the same truth with me, cleave to your companions; I will seek my own. I do this not selfishly, but humbly and truly. It is alike your interest, and mine, and all men's, however long we have dwelt in lies, to live in truth. Does this sound harsh to-day? You will soon love what is dictated by your nature as well as mine, and, if we follow the truth, it will bring us out safe at last.'—But so you may give these friends pain. Yes, but I cannot sell my liberty and my power, to save their sensibility. Besides, all persons have their moments of reason, when they look out into the region of absolute truth; then will they justify me, and do the same thing.

Having cast the question of intimacy as merely a question of self-reliance for his essays, Emerson still had to confront the problem of individualism in his own marriage. For in spite of whatever affection he felt for Lidian, his dispute with Fuller had harped too much on the virtues of individualism, and now his journals ring with criticisms and doubts about marriage's practicability. During the time when his debate with Fuller and Sturgis had still been raging, he had written in his journal, "I marry you for better, not for *worse*, I marry impersonally," and while his essays were defining the individual's self-reliance, his journals recorded serious misgivings about matrimony, for he could not ignore the fact that the spiritualized marriage he imagined remained susceptible to the tides of new attractions.

> All loves, all friendships are momentary. *Do you love me?* means at last *Do you see the same truth I see?* If you do, we are happy together: but when presently one of us passes into the perception of new truth, we are divorced and the force of all nature cannot hold us to each other. I well know how delicious is this cup we call Love,—I existing for you, you existing for me,—but it is a child's apotheosis of his toy; it is an attempt to fix & eternize the fireside & nuptial chamber, to fasten & enlarge these fugitive clouds of circumstance…In vain & in vain…
>
> But one to one, married & chained through the eternity of Ages, is frightful beyond the binding of dead & living together, & is no more conceivable to the soul than the permanence of our little platoon of gossips, Uncles, Aunts, & cousins. No, Heaven is the marriage of all souls…
>
> It is only when you leave & lose me by casting yourself on a noble sentiment which is higher than both of us that I draw near to you & find myself at your side. And I leave you & am repelled the moment you fix your eye on me & demand my love. In fact in the spiritual world we seem to change sexes every moment. You love the worth that is in me therefore I am your husband but it is not me but the worth that really fixes your love: well, that which is in me is but a drop of the Ocean of Worth that is behind me. Meantime I adore the greater worth that is in another; so I become his wife & he again aspires to a higher worth

which dwells in another spirit & so is wife or receiver of that spirit's influence. Every soul is a Venus to every other soul.

Emerson would expand on this sublimated, hermaphroditic theory further in 1842—echoing Fuller's torment about being a woman of feminine sentiment and masculine intellect:

> A highly endowed man with good intellect & good conscience is a Man-woman & does not so much need the complement of Woman to his being, as another. Hence his relations to the sex are somewhat dislocated & unsatisfactory. He asks in Woman sometimes the Woman, sometimes the Man.

When his thoughts about marriage were not abstracted, though, they were still critical. He elaborated in a separate entry,

> Plainly marriage should be a temporary relation, it should have its natural birth, climax & decay, without violence of any kind,—violence to bind, or violence to rend. When each of two souls had exhausted the other of that good which they each held for the other, they should part in the same peace in which they met, not parting from each other, but drawn to new society. The new love is the balm to prevent a wound from forming where the old love was detached. But now we could not trust even saints & sages with a boundless liberty. For the romance of new love is so delicious, that their unfixed fancies would betray them, and they would allow themselves to confound a whim with

an instinct, the pleasure of the fancy with the dictates of the character.

In spite of his rumblings, though, Emerson remained steadfastly married, resigning himself to his relationship with Lidian—and to his children and to family—without much comment—as if they were impersonal facts of fate.

VII

In spite of the questions they raised—or even, perhaps, because of them—Emerson and Fuller remained close friends. They did not relinquish each other's friendship on account of their differences, but they both turned to their writing with renewed energy. From 1840 to 1842, they were still constantly in contact as the editorial business of *The Dial* flew back and forth between them. Fuller had taken the primary editorial role, but Emerson was one of the principals, and their letters maintained a familiar, bantering tone as they discussed submissions and arrangements with contributors and printers.

Nevertheless, doubts about marriage and relationships continued to ripple through the Emerson household, for the crisis of 1840 had taken a toll on Lidian as well. As Emerson retreated into his writing, she was more sensitive about her health, which had never been good. Ever since childhood, Lidian had lived by a Spartan regimen that allowed her only four hours sleep a night, and elevated the refusal of food to a virtue. Without any literary, passionate or otherwise creative outlet for her apprehensions, the intelligence and wit that had charmed Emerson were now manifested in depression and hypochondria. While Lidian had always been "more sensitive to suffering than to happiness," her daughter Ellen recalled that "now [after 1841] this became more true of her than ever before." She gave her time to abolition movements and reform organizations like the Society for the Prevention of Cruelty to Animals, working to alleviate others' sufferings.

Fuller had ceased to press Emerson for intimacy, but she was still part of Emerson's life, and the question of transcendental friendship and its relation with marriage still colored all their intercourse. Fuller dramatizes this tension in a remarkable journal entry of September, 1842:

> L[idian] has had a slow fever which has confined her to her chamber almost ever since I came, & I have not been attentive to her as I should have been, if I had thought she cared about it. I did not go into her room at all for a day or two, simply because I was engaged all the time and kept expecting to see her downstairs. When I *did* go in, she burst into tears at the sight of me, but laid the blame on her nerves...Presently she said something which made me suppose she thought W. passed the evenings in talking with me, & a painful feeling flashed across me...I said that I was with Ellery or H[enry] T[horeau] both of the eve[nin]gs & that W. was writing in his study.
>
> I thought it all over a little, whether I was considerate enough. As to W. I never keep him from any such duties any more than a book would.— He lives his own way, & he don't soothe the illness, or morbid feelings of a friend, because he would not wish any one to do it *for him*. It is useless to expect it; what does it signify, whether he is with

me or at his writing. L. knows perfectly well, that he has no regard for me or anyone that would make him wish to be with me, a minute longer than I could fill up his time with thoughts.

As to my being more his companion that cannot be helped, his life is in the intellect not the affections. He has affection for me, but it is because I quicken his intellect.— I dismissed it all, as a mere sick moment of L's.

Yesterday she said to me, at dinner, I have not yet been out, will you be my guide for a little walk this afternoon. I said I am engaged to walk with Mr E. but—(I was going to say, I will walk with you first,) when L. burst into tears. The family were all present, they looked at their plates. Waldo looked on the ground, but soft & serene as ever. I said "My dear Lidian, certainly I will go with you." "No! she said I do not want you to make any sacrifice, but I do feel perfectly desolate, and forlorn, and I thought if I once got out, the fresh air would do me good, and that with you, I should have courage, but go with Mr E. I will not go"

I hardly knew what to say, but I insisted on going with her, & then she insisted on going so that I might return in time for my other walk. Waldo said not a word: he retained his sweetness of look, but never offered to do the least thing. I can never admire him enough at such times; he is so true to himself. In our walk and during our ride this morn g [*sic*] L. talked so fully that I felt reassured except that I think she will always have these pains, because she has always a lurking hope that Waldo's character will alter, and that he will be capable of an intimate union; now I feel convinced that it will never be more perfect between them two. I do not believe it will be less: for he is sorely troubled by imperfections in the tie, because he dont believe in anything better.—And where he loved her first, he loves her always...I thought it was the only way, to take him for what he is, as he wishes to be taken, and though my experience has been, for that very reason, so precious to me, I dont know that I could have fortitude for it in a more intimate relation. Yet nothing could be nobler, nor more consoling than to be his wife, if one's mind were only thoroughly made up to the truth...

I suppose the whole amount of the feeling is that women cant bear to be left out of the question. And they dont see the whole truth about one like me, if they did they would understand why the brow of Muse or Priestess must wear a shade of sadness. On my side I dont remember them enough. They have so much that I have not, I cant conceive of their wishing for what I have...But when Waldo's wife, & the mother of that child that is gone thinks me the most privileged of women...it does seem a little too insulting at first blush.—And yet they are not altogether wrong.

Fuller may not have actually possessed the power Lidian attributed to her, but she imagined that she would use such power very differently if she did have it. In 1842, when her sister's husband Ellery Channing overstayed his visit with his lover, Fuller wrote in her journal:

> If I were Waldo's wife, or Ellery's wife, I should acquiesce in all these relations, since they needed them. I should expect the same feeling from my husband, & I should think it little in him not to have it.

Emerson, however, would not submit his marriage to questioning—he remained closely bound with Lidian in spite of the 'imperfections in their tie,' and in spite of having lost their first son, in 1842, to scarlet fever. Little Waldo's death weighed on Emerson and Lidian together, and when Lidian wrote in Waldo's journal, in the late 1840s, "Dear husband, I wish I had never been born. I do not see how God can compensate me for the sorrow of existence," he resigned himself, and bore the burden with his wife. In early 1850, he wrote in his journal, finally settling the question:

> Love is temporary and ends in marriage. Marriage is the perfection which love aimed at, ignorant of what it sought. Marriage is a good known only to the parties. A relation of perfect understanding, aid, contentment, possession of themselves and of the world— which dwarfs love to green fruit.

VIII

AFTER 1842, EMERSON TURNED HIS FOCUS TO HIS CAREER. He published a second book of essays in 1844, and now he began to be more and more in demand, so that by 1846 he was lecturing more than fifty times a year—up to as many as eighty in the early '50s—and after the mid-1840s, he was traveling further and further for his lectures. Fuller began to strike out into new society as well. As early as October 20, 1840—just days before Emerson's final letter ended their dispute about their friendship—she had started to look beyond Concord—and even beyond herself. She had written to Caroline Sturgis,

> Like [the holy Mother] I long to be virgin. I would fly from the land of my birth. I would hide myself in night and poverty. Does a star point out the spot. The gifts I must receive, yet for my child, not me. I have no words, wait till he is of age, then hear *him*[.]
>
> Oh Caroline, my soul swells with the future. The past, I know it not...
>
> All the souls I ever loved are holy to me, their voices sound more and more sweet yet oh for an hour of absolute silence, dedicated, enshrined in the bosom of the One.

Fuller had stayed in Boston, running Conversations courses for women, and editing *The Dial* till 1842. When she gave up editorship of *The Dial*, it was for a wider experience: she traveled to Niagara Falls in 1843, and then to the Great Lakes, immersing herself in sights and observing other women's situations, as wives, as workers and as thinkers. She would publish her insights as *Summer on the Lakes* and *Woman in the Nineteenth Century*, two formative works of the women's rights movement.

After her travels in the West, Fuller moved from Boston to New York, to work on Horace Greeley's *Herald Tribune* as the paper's first female correspondent. While she was living with Greeley and his family, Fuller had a brief intimacy with a German Jew named James Nathan, but now instead of sharing abstracted passions, she came right to the point, and stated her needs. In a letter, she asked Nathan whether he was her "guardian to domesticate me in the body, and attach it more firmly to the earth?...Am I to be rooted on earth, ah! choose for me a good soil and a sunny place, that I may be a green shelter to the weary and bear fruit enough to pay for staying." Perhaps not surprisingly, Nathan took her plea for a proposition, and her next letter expressed her shock: "You have said there is in yourself both a lower and a higher than I was aware of. Since you said this, I suppose I have seen that lower!" Fuller and Nathan remained close, but the transcendental promise was gone from their friendship, and Nathan left New York before they could bring their friendship to any fruition.

Investing herself in her writing and in society, Fuller wrote to her brother in 1845, "I want that my friends should *wish* me now to act in my public career rather than towards them personally. I have given almost all my young energies to personal relations. I no longer feel inclined to this, and wish to share and impel the general stream of thought." Later that year, she departed for Europe and with her friends the Storys, she toured through Scotland, England, France and Italy, where she met Carlyle, Wordsworth, George Sand, Guiseppi Mazzini, the exiled Italian revolutionary, and Adam Mickiewicz, the exiled Polish revolutionary. Mickiewicz identified the heart of her problems when he wrote to her that "for you the first step of your deliverance…is to know whether you are to be permitted to remain a virgin."

Fuller's sexual deliverance arrived in the shape of Giovanni Ossoli, whom she met on a sightseeing trip in Rome in 1847: he helped her find her way when she was separated from her friends. Ossoli's family was not very wealthy, but he was an Italian Count, and he treated Fuller with great chivalry. In Fuller's friend Emelyn Story's account, Ossoli's "manner toward Margaret was devoted and lover-like to a striking degree—He cared not how trivial was the service if he might perform it for her." Ossoli was the youngest brother in his family, and he had been charged with taking care of their ailing father, who had died shortly before Fuller met him—if he was liberated from the role of caretaker, he was also lonely after his father's death. As Fuller would write, later, to her sister Ellen, "Our meeting was singular, fateful I may say. Very soon he offered me his hand through life, but I never dreamed I should take it. I loved him and felt very unhappy to leave him, but the connexion seemed so every way unfit, I did not hesitate a moment."

Having refused Ossoli, Fuller was still looking for deliverance, and even within a month of meeting Ossoli in Rome, she wrote to invite another man into her life. Fuller's biographers speculated that this letter and others had been written to Ossoli, but it was American painter Thomas Hicks to whom Fuller was writing:

> You are the only one whom I have seen here [in Rome] in whose eye I recognized one of my own kindred. I want to know and to love you and to have you love me...How can you let me pass you by, without full and free communication. I do not understand it, unless you are occupied by some other strong feeling. Very soon I must go from here, do not let me go without giving me some of your life. I wish this for both our sakes, for mine, because I have so lately been severed from congenial companionship, that I am suffering for want of it, for yours because I feel as if I had something precious to leave in your charge.
>
> When we are together, it does not seem to me, as if you were insensible to all this?

Two weeks later, Hicks responded, "Do you not see that I cannot make you happy? May I hope not to offend you in writing so?"

THE DANGERS OF PASSION

Rebuffed by Hicks, Fuller left Rome for further travels in Italy, but she returned to Rome and to Ossoli in October of 1847. She set up housekeeping more as a resident than as a tourist, and she wrote to her brother that she was "so happy here alone and free." As her brother was "breaking an engagement" himself, she advised him to "keep free of false ties they are the curse of life," but Fuller would not remain free for long. She must have taken Ossoli for a lover within a few months of her return, because she was pregnant with a baby boy who would be born in the beginning of September, 1848.

A letter to Caroline Sturgis—written in January, when she must have been discovering her pregnancy—indicates that she despaired at the prospect, even though she does not name her predicament:

> When I arrived in Rome, I was at first intoxicated to be here…and many circumstances combined to place me in a kind of passive, childlike well-being. That is all over now, and, with this year, I enter upon a sphere of my destiny so difficult, that I, at present, see no way out, except through the gate of death. It is useless to write of it; you are at a distance and cannot help me…I have no reason to hope I shall not reap what I have sown, and do not. Yet how I shall endure it I cannot guess; it is all a dark, sad enigma. The beautiful forms of art charm no more, and a love, in which there is all fondness, but no help, flatters in vain. I am all alone; nobody around me sees any of this.

Perhaps out of shame, or perhaps simply for privacy, Fuller was not clear about her situation, and Sturgis does not appear to have read between the lines, to recognize the gravity of Fuller's feelings. She had heard Fuller express this kind of despair about her solitude on many occasions already—she did not ask her to clarify.

Emerson had been lecturing in England in 1848, when one state after another, from Denmark to France to Poland and Italy, entered a state of political turmoil, inspired by America's revolutionary ideals. In an atmosphere of widespread turmoil and possible danger—and without knowing anything about Fuller's pregnancy—he wrote to her in May, offering to escort her home. The Italian states had just established a new political unity, though, and were preparing to wage a war of independence from Austria, and she refused: "I should like to return with you, but I have much to do and learn in Europe yet. I am deeply interested in this public drama, and wish to see it played out. Methinks I have my part therein, either as actor or historian." Emerson returned home without seeing her in her pregnancy or ever meeting her husband, and he never saw Fuller playing her part in the short-lived Italian Republic.

Fuller had not told Emerson—or anyone—about her pregnancy, so when she left Rome for the country in May, she hid her motives by saying that she was going away to work on a history of the Italian Revolution. She gave birth to a baby boy in Rieti in September, but she was anxious to come back to

Rome, where the political turmoil was tending toward Italian self-rule, and where Ossoli was becoming active in the Republican militia. When she returned to Rome, she left her baby with a nurse who received money so irregularly that she threatened to abandon him.

Fuller covered the Italian Revolution for the *Herald Tribune*, but the tumult of the Revolution obfuscated her actions so well that even now it remains impossible to tell when, where or even whether she and Ossoli were married. Some have speculated that Ossoli would have had difficulty getting a Papal dispensation to marry outside of his faith. Still others have said they kept the marriage secret because Ossoli stood to lose his share of his father's estate if it were known that he had married a Protestant. Others have said that there was no wedding at all. Not a few people have noted that a fatalism must have pervaded their entire relationship, for in Emelyn Story's account, Fuller returned to Rome when a siege by French troops was inevitable: she gave her letters to friends for safekeeping, and helped run a hospital while the fighting intensified. When she joined Ossoli at his forward post—which "was one of considerable danger...being in one of the most exposed places," Story said—she reports that Fuller had said she did not expect to survive.

Nonetheless, Fuller, Ossoli and their baby all came safely through the siege, and the subsequent defeat of the Republican forces. In the aftermath of the defeat, Fuller began to write to friends, mentioning Ossoli and her baby openly. But even when she wrote to her sister Ellen in December, she was still only sketching:

> About [Ossoli] I do not like to say much, as he is an exceedingly delicate person. He is not precisely reserved, but it is not natural to him to *talk* about the objects of strong affection...I expect that, to many of my friends Mr. Emerson for one, he will be nothing, and they will not understand that I should have life in common with him. But I do not think he will care; he has not the slightest tinge of self-love; he has throughout our intercourse been used to my having many such ties; he has no wish to be anything to persons with whom he does not feel spontaneously bound, and when I am occupied is happy in himself ...should he continue to love me as he has done, to consider his companionship will be an inestimable blessing to me. I say *if*, because all human affections are frail, and I have experienced too great revulsions in my own not to know it, yet I feel great confidence in the permanence of his love...he is capable of the sacred love, the love passing that of woman, he showed it to his father, to Rome, to me...
>
> I acted upon a strong impulse. I could not analyze at all what passed in my mind. I neither rejoice nor grieve, for bad or for good, I acted out my character...As to marriage I think the intercourse of heart and mind may be fully enjoyed without entering into this partnership of daily life, still I do not find it burdensome. We get along very well

and I find have our better intercourse as much as if we did not buy (unhappily we have nothing to sell) together…

Still all this I had felt before in some degree. The great novelty, the immense gain to me is my relation with my child. I thought the mother's heart lived in me before, but it did not. I knew nothing about it. Yet before his birth I dreaded it…When he was born that deep melancholy turned at once into rapture, but it did not last long, then came the prudential motherhood…I became a coward, a caretaker not only for the morrow but impiously faithless twenty or thirty years ahead. It seemed wicked to have brought the tender little thing into the midst of cares and complexities…

When I saw his first smile, new resolution dawned in my heart, I resolved to live day by day and hour by hour for his dear sake and feed on ashes when offered. So if he is only treasure lent, if he must go as sweet Waldo did…I shall at least have these days and hours with him…

My love to dear E[lizabet]h I wish she and Mr Emerson would write to me, but I suppose they dont know what to say. Tell them there is no need to say anything about these affairs if they dont want to. I am just the same for them I was before.

Fuller was married, now, but she did not pretend that she had made a perfect match. When she finally broke the news to her mother in 1849, she wrote that Ossoli was

not in any respect such a person as people in general would expect to find with me. He had no instructor except an old priest, who entirely neglected his education; and of all that is contained in books he is absolutely ignorant, and he has no enthusiasm of character.

If Ossoli could not share her intellectual work, though, he still left her free, and Fuller told her mother that she had "found a home, and one that interferes with no tie." Having harbored doubts about marriage, she expressed some uncertainty about the permanence of Ossoli's love as well:

> I do not know whether he will always love me so well, for I am the elder, and the difference will become, in a few years, more perceptible than now. But life is so uncertain, and it is so necessary to take good things without their limitations, that I have not thought it worth while to calculate too curiously.

Plagued by poverty in the post-revolution city, where Ossoli had difficulties finding work, Fuller and Ossoli decided to return to America, where they would have an easier time supporting themselves and their son. But returning home was a daunting prospect as well, for now Fuller would have to explain not only her conflicting stories about her travels, but her original silence about her husband and baby son. Emerson recalled the atmosphere of intense speculation that surrounded their return:

> The timorous said, What shall we do? how shall she be received, now that she brings a husband & child home? But she had only to open her mouth, & a triumphant success awaited her. She would fast enough have disposed of the

circumstances & the bystanders. For she had the impulse, & they wanted it. Here were already mothers waiting tediously for her coming, for the education of their daughters.

The questions were never answered by her arrival. Fuller, Ossoli and their child all died when a hurricane caught their schooner off the coast of Long Island; it broke up on a sand bar fifty yards from the Fire Island shore, and Fuller was last seen clinging to the mast. Emerson dispatched Henry David Thoreau to the scene of the wreck, but neither Fuller's nor Ossoli's bodies were recovered—Nino alone received a formal burial. Told of Fuller's death, Emerson wrote in his journal: "I have lost in her my audience. I hurry now to my work admonished that I have few days left."

IX

EMERSON WAS ORIGINALLY DAUNTED BY THE PROSPECT of a literary memorial. He wrote to his English friend Thomas Carlyle,

> I think it could really be done, if one would heroically devote himself, and a most vivacious book written, but it must be done *tête exaltée*, & in the tone of Spiridon, or even of Bettine, with the coolest ignoring of...Mr Willis Mr Carlyle and Boston and London...Nay...I think, when the first experiments came to be made, it might turn out to be a work above our courage.

Nonetheless, with Channing and Clarke, he began to organize a volume in tribute to Fuller. Sam Ward had begged off: "How can you describe a force?" he asked. "How can you write a life of Margaret?" to which Emerson had replied that "the question itself is some description of her." Emerson, Clarke and Channing edited her journals and letters, but they neglected to solicit testimonials from Mickiewicz or other of Fuller's European friends, so the *Memoirs* remained a thoroughly American portrait of a woman who had only finally fulfilled her fate in Europe.

Fuller's death gave Emerson access to all her journals—it was as close as they would come to a consummation—but the portrait that emerged in the *Memoirs* was hardly flattering. Emerson recalled that "the men thought [Fuller] carried too many guns, and the women did not like one who despised them. I believe I fancied her too much interested in personal history." He wrote that "she made me laugh more than I liked" and now he found "something profane in the hours of amusing gossip into which she drew me." He confided in his journal, in 1851 that

> the unlooked for trait in all these journals to me is the Woman, poor woman: they are all hysterical. She is bewailing her virginity and languishing for a husband. 'I need help. No, I need a full, a godlike embrace from some sufficient love.' &c. &c....This I doubt not was all the more violent recoil from the exclusively literary & 'educational' connections in which she had lived.

Elsewhere in the *Memoirs*, Emerson wrote,

> when I found she lived at a rate so much faster than mine, and which was violent compared with mine, I foreboded rash and painful crises, and had a feeling as if a voice cried, *Stand from under!*—as if, a little further on, this destiny was threatened with jars and reverses, which no friendship could avert or console...She remained inscrutable to me; her strength was not my strength,—her powers were a surprise.

The years that had passed since their quarrel, and all of Fuller's development in Europe, had not brought Emerson to see the fire she complained his light could not comprehend. He confessed in the *Memoirs*, "I did not know, as a friend should know, to prize a silence as much as a discourse," and he could see that "a forlorn feeling was [therefore] inevitable." "As I did not understand [her] discontent then," he elaborated, "of course I cannot now. It was a war of temperaments, and could not be reconciled by words."

This intransigent resignation was not Emerson's last word on Fuller, though. She persisted in his thinking, and his grief for her survives in his 1860 essay "Fate," where her ghost appears in his metaphor for fate: "we must see that the world is rough and surly, and will not mind drowning a man or a woman, but swallows your ship like a grain of dust." Over time, Emerson even began to deify Fuller a little. By 1866, he came to wonder whether

> Margaret with her radiant genius & fiery heart was perhaps the real centre that drew so many & so various individuals to a seeming union. Hedge, Clarke, W. H. Channing, W. E. Channing, jr. [sic], George Ripley, James Clarke & many more then or since known as writers, or otherwise distinguished, were only held together as her friends.

This strange magnetic force of Fuller's had never been more than an impersonal power in Emerson's view, and Emerson himself had always been threatened by the possibility that he might have responded to her with a personal force of his own.

But by the time he met Fuller, Emerson had already lost his first love, and he had already chosen his second wife, and had children with her. Marriage was an almost exclusively spiritual experience in his journals and letters—as he wrote in his journal in 1852, "everything is free but marriage": it was a fateful event that could not be changed, and in spite of his private doubts about the institution, he did not feel free to look beyond it.

After 1841, when he wrote in his essay "Circles" that "a man's growth is seen in the successive choirs of his friends," Emerson would inspire self-reliant individuals to grow through successive relationships, but he himself could not accept a personal or spiritual progress that moved through one marriage or relationship after another. Marriage was still a chaste spiritual union, a defense against the lower instincts. "If [spouses'] wisdoms come near & meet," he wrote, "there is no danger of passion." Fully aware of his own individuality, Emerson describes passion not as a desirable state of arousal, receptivity and merging, but as the agony that comes from shared longing for an impossible union. Any actual union outside of marriage would have complicated life for him—and for everyone around him—had he pursued it. But if Emerson himself described his own temperament as icy, on account of his reaction to Fuller and others, it may have been that he was simply honoring his marriage, and keeping passion alive where he could live with it: in his writing, in his family, in his memory of Ellen and in his children.

AFTERWORD

This story was originally meant to be the first chapter of *The Love Lives of the Artists: Five Stories of Creative Intimacy*, which tells the stories of twentieth-century artists' relationships—it was not included because Emerson and Fuller never had a consummated relationship, and they never took lovers, as all the more recent couples had done. But even as I told the other stories in *Love Lives*—where artists like Anaïs Nin and Simone de Beauvoir wrote compelling and even incandescent journals that reconciled erotic freedom and commitment in marriages that transcended jealousy with shared creativity— even as the twentieth century artists made real and consequential experiments with the question of commitment and creativity, Emerson and Fuller remained heroes for me. Emerson for the carefully maintained blindness that allowed him to preserve his marriage to Lidian—Fuller for her determination to pester the old man into living out his philosophy, even in its contradictions. I am not inclined to take sides in their quarrel, which strikes me as inevitable, and merely tragic. Obviously the times were on his side more than on hers, as it would have been profoundly scandalous for him to have left Lidian, or even to have been unfaithful to her, and it is not clear that Fuller even wanted him on these terms.

I even admired—I continue to admire—the blindness with which Emerson both foresaw and refused to see the complications that would come from his intimacy with Fuller. I don't believe that there was ever a moment when Emerson and Fuller contemplated a sexual fulfillment. "You would have me love you," he wrote in his journal. "What shall I love? Your body? The supposition disgusts you." In fact, Emerson seems to have been much closer to Caroline Sturgis than Fuller. His feelings for her are only subtly discernible in his letters—but in his dispute with Fuller, he was always counting and weighing philosophical truths, without the elevated tenderness he showed to Sturgis. The debate they had—debate itself being hostile to intimacy—seems to me to describe frustrations they had in each other, certainly—but it also described frustrations they had in the world, even if they found the vocabulary of friendship and intimacy in their expression.

In the end, I think that Emerson simply lacked the words for the kind of experience Fuller or Sturgis hoped he might have. They may have wanted to see that the great philosopher was capable of suffering, or passion—perhaps they simply wanted to see that they tortured them, that they had that power. But it was not something Emerson could give them, either of them. He never saw their feelings, or never admitted seeing. But his thought was so new, and his personal authority was so great, that the image Fuller gives us, of Emerson smiling blithely, while his wife cried hysterical tears—and Fuller herself rescheduled her walk to placate her—shows us clearly enough how he skirted the passions. He had the reputation for elevated feelings—and even if they were elevated to the point of ruthlessness in his essays, he needed to preserve the sublime elevation of his household, as well.

Nevertheless, if it is Emerson's language we use—as Americans, and as moderns—for our freedom and for our responsibility to ourselves, it seems to me that it is Fuller's emotions and experiences that really resonate with us. Fuller's life shows us a tragedy we recognize as our own. She was younger than Emerson—she didn't yet have a reputation to protect. She had a name to establish—and she might have become an American Harriet Martineau, if she had been able to depart for Europe in 1835. But when her father died, intestate, life itself intervened, as it does, and she never found a secure place from which to make her own literature and philosophy. She had her life to live, and if she had known since childhood that it would be an unprecedented life, she would always be on the run, now, as she made it. But now that she was in constant motion, no single experience could have fulfilled her. She didn't just have a philosophy: she was a woman, she had that other life to live, and to account for, if she could.

Comparisons being always a little bit odious, Fuller's despair, on finding herself pregnant, unmarried and far from home, nonetheless strikes me as a greater experience than any of the deaths that touched Emerson's life. True, he had to survive with his grief, in the absence of the people he had loved, but he still had others—his mother, his Aunt Mary, his wife Lidian and his children, to help care for him—he still had his family, his home and his region. By the time she had even met Ossoli, Fuller had already given up homeland and her family, and when she realized she was pregnant, she didn't have anything but a man she hardly knew, and an identity that had just been become very real—and potentially very limiting—in its consequences. No one but traveling companions even witnessed her plight, when she realized that she was going to be responsible not only for herself and her own acts—deliberate or no, elevated or no—but she was going to be assuming responsibility as well for the life she'd created with Ossoli—her own new life, the life of their baby, and the life she had entered into in common with her new husband.

More than Emerson's grief—annihilating as it was—Fuller's despair is what seems to me to clarify the self, and to teach the lesson of self-reliance, the practice of it, in modern times. In her decision to leave for Europe—then in her leap into intimacy, and then in her leap into the consequences, in staying the course with the man she had found herself with—Fuller seems to me, much more than Emerson, to have been acting out her inner nature, and giving herself a wide field for self-knowledge, contradictions and problems notwithstanding.

When the siege of Rome did not kill her for her principles, she prepared to return to America, determined to see what trials life still had in store for her and her husband and child. I will not speculate about how or whether she would have given Ossoli his freedom, as she had imagined that she might have given Emerson or Ellery Channing theirs. But even by the brief light of her marriage and maternity, her trials were not merely trials of experience: they were trials of her philosophy, and this story of marriage and self-reliance suffers—if stories can suffer—for Fuller's untimely death. I do believe that she herself would have contributed to that story not only with her decisions but with her writing: she would have left a unique account of her new experiences.

Nevertheless, it seems to me that in Fuller's willingness to live in a present moment—richly, and tragically, if need be— she was better suited to later times—the 1890s, the Jazz age, the 1960s—when the obstacles that locked each individual into the cage of his or her own personality—and into the cage of culture as well—had come to seem all-powerful, and almost unbearable. When people began to imagine the tragic leap—into a new, unknown world—as an escape—when that leap became a modern rite of passage, it seems to me that it emerged more from Fuller's sense of tragic uniqueness, than from Emerson's self-reliance, which was forged in loss, sure, but not in the terrifying wilderness that Fuller found in Europe.

THE DANGERS OF PASSION

Whether we say that Emerson lacked the courage to make the leap that would act out his philosophy—or whether we say instead that he had the courage of prior convictions, by honoring ties to family, wife and children—it seems that at least in love, he himself was not such a self-reliant individual. If he foresaw the possibility of a "new and unprecedented way" to fulfill a marriage, his words merely resonated beyond his own experience: he inspired his readers to make experiments he himself would not make. Emerson's times may have been too early, for the kind of experimentation that would follow after him, but his language of self-reliance would still lead to all of the freedoms and power—and possibility and self-invention—that came with industrial culture. It would be up to people like Fuller—young people, restless, promising, and hungry for new kinds of fulfillment—to test his theories in their lives. So in spite of the fact that we still use Emerson's language, it seems to me that Fuller is the one in whom we really recognize a kinship, as the one who really leapt into our age, where self-reliance and marriage are still being tested against each other.

§

As modern freedoms emerged from the horse-drawn morality of the early nineteenth century—as matrimonial arrangements became grounds for experimentation along with everything else—Emerson's language—and also his quarrel with Fuller—would continue to evolve, as later writers inherited the freedoms that were just being born in Emerson's time.

Thirty years after Fuller's death, Emerson and Fuller's friendship—and their quarrel—were reprised by Friedrich Nietzsche and his relationship with Lou von Salomé. An enthusiastic follower of Emerson, Nietzsche was just preparing his mature philosophy when he met Lou von Salomé, who was twenty-one to his thirty-seven. She had already been schooled deeply in Western philosophy, and her arrival in Nietzsche's life confirmed something he had suspected might be possible. He saw Salomé as an ideal potential disciple, and Salomé herself was said to personify his philosophy. With fellow philosopher Paul Rée, who was thirty-two, Nietzsche and Salomé formed a 'winter plan' to live, study and write together, in a chaste—if sexually charged—'Trinity'.

We can hear an Emersonian self-trust in Nietzsche's insistence that the three philosophers could make their arrangements without regard for convention: "Neither Mrs. Rée in Warmbrunn," Nietzsche wrote to Salomé, "nor Miss von Meysenbug in Bayreuth [a mentor of Lou's] nor my family need break their heads and hearts over things that *we, we, we* alone are and shall be up to, whereas they may strike others as dangerous fantasies." In defending her plans from her own family's outrage, Salomé was also to use Emersonian language: "I can't live according to some model...but I intend to shape my life for myself...Let's see whether the so-called 'insurmountable barriers' life puts in most people's way don't in fact turn out to be harmless chalk lines!" Marriage itself was a merely formal institution, and as such an impediment: Nietzsche had written to Rée that "I could consent at most to a two-year marriage, and then only in view of what I mean to do these next ten years." When Nietzsche had told Salomé, early in their relationship, that he might have to offer her his hand "so as to protect you from what people might say," the misunderstanding caused some tension between them, for Salomé was outraged that sex and marriage should have any part in their tie.

If social conventions could be excluded from the Trinity, desire could not. Rée, it turned out, was in love with Salomé, and he told her that Nietzsche only wanted her for a concubine—at the same time that Nietzsche's proud and profoundly conventional sister Elizabeth was warning Nietzsche against Salomé and her "raging egoism." After only seven months' intimacy, Nietzsche was infuriated by Rée's betrayal, and poisoned by his sister's condemnations, and he broke with Rée and Salomé together: he would follow their careers and read their books, but they would never be reunited. He launched into his own writing, and his *Genealogy of Morals* and *Also Sprach Zarathustra* can be read partly as lectures in morality to Rée and Salomé. He did not seek out other lovers—he immersed himself in his writing until he was forced by his health to stop in 1889.

The Transcendental Friendship of Ralph Waldo Emerson & Margaret Fuller

If Nietzsche followed Emerson into chastity and literature, Salomé followed Fuller in inventing the relationships that would fulfill her. When her friendship with Nietzsche collapsed, Salomé and Rée recruited other writers to be part of other chaste Trinities. Like Fuller, Salomé's marriage was unconventional, for when she did finally marry, at twenty-six—to a Persian scholar fifteen years older than her—she never consummated the bond. Her husband had a child with the housekeeper, and Lou herself took a succession of lovers—artists and psychologists who were younger than her by eight to eighteen years. Fifty years, now, after Fuller, Salomé had the freedom Fuller had imagined for herself, and she lived long enough to see her influence bear fruit in the career of the poet Rainer Maria Rilke, who was both inspired and steadied by his sexual relationship with Salomé—which never, it should be said, excluded other ties. Rilke himself would follow Salomé's example as well, and abandon his wife and child after less than a year and half of marriage: he would take a succession of lovers, without honoring any tie but to his work, and the personal development that took place there.

The question of creative self-reliance and marriage had evolved further by the time it came around again in the 1930s, in the relationship between Henry Miller and Anaïs Nin. For now, instead of faltering on conventional morality and the threat of sex, like Nietzsche and Salomé, Miller and Nin celebrated their 'diabolical' and 'infernal' relationship: their writing described their numerous adulterous relationships as the new paradigm for marriage in a modern world that was decaying toward death. Miller and Nin had inherited Nietzsche and Freud and their followers' vocabularies for the warring oppositions within the psyche, but they still retained the idea of a self-reliant intuition and individuality, which Emerson had described as the sole arbiter of moral reasoning and experience. They both used their writing—as much as their lives themselves—to 'act out their characters,' insisting on even their destructive desires. This ability—to turn their characters into a revealing literature of self-destruction and transformation—had become the only virtue.

In the end, though, Miller and Nin's relationship did not escape from the tensions Emerson and Fuller had felt, between loyalty to one's own ongoing development, and loyalty to something like marriage. Miller himself turned away from the chaos inherent in self-fulfillment: when he found out in January of 1935 that Nin had deceived him about having traveled to New York with her therapist, Otto Rank—instead of with her husband, as she told him—Miller made the leap back to marriage. "Your body burns in me," he wrote, "and I want it uniquely, for myself alone. That is the mistake I made—to share you." The emotional chaos of multiple relationships was no longer proof of their philosophical or psychological genuineness: now Miller wanted something beyond self-fulfillment, and when his relationship with Nin finally collapsed a few years later, he married and started a family in California. Even though he divorced this wife, and married again several times, he was living a more or less monogamous life, now, protecting his time and his peace for writing in a way that Emerson might have recognized.

Nin, on the other hand, took Fuller and Salomé's legacies to the extreme, in defining her own terms for marriage and self-fulfillment. Having been sexually involved with her father as a young girl—and having received a sporadic education in numerous European cities, before she returned to America with her mother and brothers at age eleven—without formal training in philosophy, she used sex and her own emotional life as her tools for self-discovery. Shortly after she and her Scottish banker husband, Hugo Guiler, moved to Paris, her strict Catholic upbringing yielded to sexual license, and she created an artistic identity that testified unapologetically to her sexual experiences in her journal, and sexual infidelity became a form of self-lacerating devotion to creativity. Starting in 1931, she took Miller and her therapists and her homosexual cousin and countless other men as lovers, and when a younger lover, Rupert Pole, insisted on marriage in 1955, she did not have scruples about her marriage to Guiler: for eleven years, she simply preserved the appearances that would satisfy both of her husbands. Bigamy strained her psyche, but even when she was pulled apart by her affairs, she insisted that she was still following her own development. "God, I hate myself," she wrote in her journal, "And yet I am happy, healthy."

If the question of love and self-reliance was no closer to being settled in practical terms for Emerson and Fuller's rhapsodic correspondence and then their quarrel—and then for Nietzsche and Salomé's or Henry Miller and Anaïs Nin's subsequent experiments—its evolution over time did raise the stakes, so that the terms became diabolical in Miller and Nin's writings. Marriage remained the same renunciation of sexual explorations—but now the sadomasochism in Nin's affairs and the contradictions and inconsistencies in her journals—in addition to her constant lies and her nervous breakdowns—measured the psychological cost of self-fulfillment outside of marriage.

Even still, even now, the question has to be asked anew by every individual who feels a conflict in their obligations—to spouse or lover, to the self and its development. Indeed, the consequences themselves have to be discovered anew as every individual weighs the costs of whatever fulfillment they find, for fulfillment, it would seem, must always have a cost. As industrialism continues to evolve, people are being born into more and more freedom, but the wisdom that comes from the use of this freedom is harder to pass down, if it can be passed down at all. In the hundred and seventy years since Emerson and Fuller's friendship reached its crisis, the literature of self-reliance in love has found further expression, in Sartre and Beauvoir, in Miller and Nin, and in other couples who've written about their fidelities and infidelities. But it is not clear that modern freedoms have changed the soul itself—for every generation since Emerson and Fuller has had to balance their expanding freedoms and powers against the strict and unrelenting pressure, inside of the soul, for something like chastity, or self-transcendence—for something like marriage.

PERMISSIONS

The author would like to thank the Ralph Waldo Emerson Memorial Association deposit, Houghton Library, Harvard University, for permission to reprint excerpts from Ralph Waldo Emerson's Margaret Fuller notebook, call number MS Am 1280H (111).

Image of Ralph Waldo Emerson courtesy of the Concord Free Public Library.

Image of Margaret Fuller courtesy of Cambridge Historical Commission.

ATTRIBUTIONS

vii "I will have no covenants…" (*Portable Emerson*. Carl Bode, ed. New York: Penguin Books, 1981. p. 154).

"No old form suits me…" (*Memoirs of Margaret Fuller Ossoli*. Boston: Roberts Brothers, 1881. Volume I, 297—hereinafter *Memoirs*).

2 "a good husband…" (Chevigny, Bell Gale. *Margaret Fuller: The Woman and the Myth*. Boston: Northeastern University Press, 1994. p. 235—hereinafter *The Woman and the Myth*).

4 "discern the law by which [she was] filling [her] circle." (*The Woman and the Myth*, 124).

"*in spite of real sorrows.*" (*Portable Emerson*, 10).

6 "enjoy an original relation…" (*Portable Emerson*, 7)

7 "I had no natural childhood." (*Memoirs*, I, 15).

8 "untiring in his industry…" (*Memoirs*, I, 361).

"Everything [about the Romans]…" (*Memoirs*, I 18).

"I was taught Latin…" (*Memoirs*, I, 17).

9 "a man of business…" (*The Woman and the Myth*, 37).

"feelings were kept on the stretch…" (*Memoirs*, I, 15).

10 "did me good, for by them…" (*Memoirs*, I, 31).

"I had no success in associating…" (*Memoirs*, I, 41).

THE DANGERS OF PASSION

"Duty was her daily food..." (*The Woman and the Myth*, 20).

11 "rather degraded from Cicero..." (Chipperfield, Faith. *In Quest of Love: The Life and Death of Margaret Fuller*. New York: Coward McCann, 1957. p. 59).

"a strange bird...there..." (Fuller, Margaret. *Portable Margaret Fuller*. New York: Penguin Books, 1994. p. 119).

12 "so precocious..." (*The Woman and the Myth*, 30).

"one of those 'Whom men love not...'" (*Portable Margaret Fuller*, 128).

"trained to great dexterity in artificial methods..." (*Memoirs*, I, 17).

"addressed her not as a plaything..." (*The Woman and the Myth*, 249).

13 "piety, purity, submissiveness, and domesticity." (Welter, 152).

"as women have none of the objects..." (Martineau, Harriet. *Society in America*. London: Unders & Otley, 1837. p. 292).

14 "feminine receptiveness..." (*The Woman and the Myth*, 31).

"at Cambridge she had drawn..." *(Memoirs,* I, 205).

For Timothy Fuller's political history seeChipperfield, *In Quest of Love*, p. 89.

16 "already beheld many times the youth..." (*Memoirs*, I, 205).

"beings born under the same star..." (*Memoirs*, I, 37).

"I study much… (Fuller, Margaret. *The Letters of Margaret Fuller*, Robert N. Hudspeth, ed., Ithaca: Cornell University Press, 1983-1995. Volume I, page 153.).

17 "large-brained Woman…" (*Memoirs*, I, 33-35).

18 "an almost maternal friendship," (*Memoirs*, I, 299).

"undertook to mould [Fuller]…" (*The Woman and the Myth*, 69).

"I sigh for an intellectual guide…" (*The Woman and the Myth*, 56).

19 "favorite son of a [self-made] Boston banker" (*In Quest of Love*, 113).

22 For Emerson's family, see Richardson, Allen, Bosco & Myerson, Porte, etc.

23 "Genius always new…" (Bosco, Ronald A. and Joel Myerson. *The Emerson Brothers: A Fraternal Biography in Letters*. New York: Oxford University Press, 2006. p. 21).

"Give me, my God, to know…" (Richardson, Robert. *Emerson: The Mind on Fire*. Berkeley, University of California Press, 1995. p. 26).

"accounted by the near relatives…" (Haskins, David Greene. *Ralph Waldo Emerson: His maternal ancestors, with some reminiscences of him*. Port Washington, NY: Kennikat Press, 1971. p. 51).

24 For more about Everett, see Chipperfield, 68-73.

25 "very beautiful by universal consent..." (Emerson, Ellen Tucker. *One First Love: The Letters of Ellen Louisa Tucker to Ralph Waldo Emerson."* Edith Gregg, ed. Boston: Harvard University Press, 1962. p. 5).

26 "we were *acquainted*..." (*One First Love*, 38).

"I love you dearly Waldo." (*One First Love*, 51).

"These lovers are blind..." (Allen, Gay Wilson. *Waldo Emerson: A Biography*. New York: Viking, 1991. p. 144).

27 "every pain [as] a scourge..." (*One First Love*, 2).

"she is too lovely to live long..." (Pommer, Henry. *Emerson's First Marriage*. Carbondale: Southern Illinois University Press, 1967. p. 13).

28 "sharpened into anguish...'" (*Emerson: The Mind on Fire*, 108).

"My angel is gone..." (*Emerson's Letters*, I, 318).

29 "made but one man together." (*The Emerson Brothers*, 6).

31 "In the death of my son..." (*Portable Emerson*, 269).

"In the presence of nature..." (*Portable Emerson*, 10).

32 "The foregoing generations..." (*Portable Emerson*, 7).

33 "singular looking person..." (*Life of Lidian*, 49).

"what Father admired in her...'" (*Life of Lidian*, 51).

34 "what Mr Emerson said..." (*Life of Lidian* , 47).

"There are some occult facts..." (*Journals and Miscellaneous Notes*, Emerson, Ralph Waldo, William H. Gilman, ed., Cambridge: Belknap Press, 1960-82, Volume V, p. 82— hereinafter *JMN*).

35 "The strict limits..." (*Waldo Emerson: A Biography*, 240).

"was utterly amazed..." (*Life of Lidian*, 48).

36 "she could not call Father..." (*Life of Lidian*, 51).

"the tremendous manner..." (*Life of Lidian*, 48).

"very sober joy" *(Emerson's Letters*, 1: 436).

37 "In life all finding..." (Porte, Joel. *Emerson in his Journals*. Cambridge: Belknap Press, 1982, 160 [April 12-15 1836]).

"Lidian...magnanimously..." (*Emerson's First Marriage*, 91).

38 "Now began what Mother..." (*Life of Lidian*, 79).

39 "hospitably disposed," (*Life of Lidian*, 71).

"put a poster out at the gate..." (*Life of Lidian*, 71).

"whole books of Homer's *Iliad*." (*In Quest of Love*, 70).

For more about the Transcendental Club, see Richardson, 245, ff.

40 "Never speak of sin..." (*Life of Lidian*, 81).

41 "Of personal influence..." (*Memoirs*, I, 298).

"She is quite an extraordinary person..." (*Emerson's Letters*, II, 32).

"a holiday, and so was her abode..." (*Memoirs*, I, 213).

42 "Emerson's influence has been..." (*The Woman and the Myth*, 122).

"I believe I had the pleasure..." (*Memoirs*, I, 204).

43 "I think it perfectly true... (*The Woman and the Myth*, 518).

"It seems to me she is the only..." (*Emerson's Letters*, II, 210).

44 "I found no dulness in it..." (*Emerson's Letters*, 142).

"I know that not possibly..." (*Emerson's Letters*, 197).

"I do not think I shall be..." (*Emerson's Letters*, II, 226).

"power of bringing out Mr. Emerson..." (*The Woman and the Myth*, 90).

45 "a life of Margaret is impossible..." (*Memoirs*, I, 205).

"a sincerely good visit from Caroline Sturgis..." (*Emerson's Letters*, II, 205).

"I would not on any account have failed to see..." (*Emerson's Letters*, II, 228).

46 "lady who knew her well..." (*Memoirs*, I, 281).

See Rusk, Volume II, for Emerson's more rhapsodic letters.

"what were we born to do: and how shall we do it?" (*The Woman and the Myth*, 211).

47 "not to multiply books, but to report life"—(*The Woman and the Myth*, 153)

"You are as good—it may be better than ever..." (*Emerson's Letters*, II, 238).

"A little impatient...(*Emerson's Letters*, II, 238).

"most of the persons whom I..." (*Emerson in his Journals*, 230).

48 "We will be equal to an Idea..." (*Emerson's Letters*, II, 242).

"I...startled my mother & my wife..." (*Emerson's Letters*, II, 245).

49 "It is so true that a woman may be in love with a woman..." (*The Woman and the Myth*, 113).

50 "We were truly friends, but..." (*Memoirs*, I, 98-101).

51 "I know I have never been anything but a child..." (*Emerson: The Mind on Fire*, 328).

52 "I thought [Barker] had looked the world through..." (*Emerson: The Mind on Fire*, 327).

"I am bent on being his only friend myself..." (*The Woman and the Myth*, 76).

53 "[Margaret] and C[aroline]. would gladly be my friends..." (*JMN*, VII, 509).

"I dare not engage my peace so far..." (*Emerson's Letters*, II, 325).

54 "I hate everything frugal..." (*Emerson's Letters*, II, 326).

56 "You would have me love you. What shall I love?..." (*JMN*, VII, 400).

"Since I have been an exile so long..." (*Emerson's Letters*, II, 332).

"I will identify you with the Ideal Friend..." (*Emerson's Letters*, II, 334).

57 "In your last letter…you…do say…" (*Emerson's Letters*, II, 336-337).

"I have felt the impossibility…" (*The Woman and the Myth*, 124).

59 "When I write a letter to any one…" (*JMN*, VII, 404-405).

60 "Waldo is still only a small…" (Fuller, Margaret. *The Letters of Margaret Fuller*. Robert N. Hudspeth, ed. Ithaca: Cornell University Press, 1983-1994. Volume II, p. 170).

"A strong passion or…" (*Emerson's Letters*, II, 349).

"I ought never to have…" (*Emerson's Letters*, II, 352).

63 "They say in heaven…" (*Emerson's Letters*, Letters, II, 438).

"I say to myself, it is surely very generous…" (*Emerson's Letters*, II, 464).

64 "I do not look on myself as a valuable…" (Sams, Henry. *Autobiography of Brook Farm*. Englewood Cliffs: Prentice-Hall, 1958. p. 11).

"Live no longer to the expectation of these…" (*Portable Emerson*, 154, 160).

65 "I marry you for better…" (*Emerson's Letters*, VII, 336).

66 "All loves, all friendships are momentary…" (*JMN*, VII, 532-533).

67 "A highly endowed man with good intellect…" (*JMN*, VIII, 175).

"it is not in the plan or prospect of the soul…" (*JMN*, VIII, 34).

"Plainly marriage should be a temporary relation..." (*JMN*, VIII, 95).

69 "more sensitive to suffering..." (*Life of Lidian*, 83).

70 "L[idian] has had a slow fever..." (*The Woman and the Myth*, 127-128).

73 "If I were Waldo's wife, or Ellery's wife..." (*The Woman and the Myth*, 131).

"so far as union of one with one is believed to be..." (*The Woman and the Myth*, 253).

"Dear husband, I wish I had never been born..." (*Emerson: The Mind on Fire*, 390).

"Love is temporary and ends in marriage..." (*Emerson in his Journals*, 409).

74 "Like [the holy Mother] I long to be virgin..." (*The Woman and the Myth*, 523).

75 "guardian to domesticate me in the body..." (*Love Letters of Margaret Fuller*, 20-21).

"You have said there is in yourself..." (*Love Letters of Margaret Fuller*, 24).

76 "I want that my friends should *wish*..." (*The Woman and the Myth*, 135).

"For you the first step of your deliverance..." (*The Woman and the Myth*, 300).

"manner toward Margaret was devoted and lover-like..." (*The Woman and the Myth*, 409).

THE DANGERS OF PASSION

77 "Our meeting was singular, fateful I may say…" (*The Woman and the Myth*, 487).

"You are the only one whom I have seen here…" (*The Woman and the Myth*, 425).

"Do you not see that I cannot make you happy?…" (*The Woman and the Myth*, 424).

78 "breaking an engagement…" (*The Woman and the Myth*, 434).

"When I arrived in Rome, I was at first intoxicated…" (*The Woman and the Myth*, 441).

79 "I should like to return with you…" (*The Woman and the Myth*, 453).

80 "post was one of considerable danger…" (*The Woman and the Myth*, 408).

81 "About [Ossoli] I do not like to say much…" (*The Woman and the Myth*, 489).

82 "not in any respect such a person…" (*The Woman and the Myth*, 484).

"I do not know whether he…" (*The Woman and the Myth*, 484).

83 "The timorous said, What shall we do?…" (*Emerson in his Journals*, 414; Journals, July/Aug 1850).

84 "I have lost in her my audience…" (*Emerson in his Journals*, 414).

85 "I think it could really be done..." (*Margaret Fuller: The Woman and the Myth*, 415).

"How can you describe a force?..." (*Emerson: The Mind on Fire*, 484).

86 "the men thought she carried too many guns..." (*Memoirs*, I, 202).

"When I found she lived at a rate..." (*Memoirs*, I, 228-229).

"I did not know, as a friend..." (*Memoirs*, I, 288).

"The unlooked for trait in..." (*Emerson in his Journals*, 414).

"we must see that the world..." (*Portable Emerson*, 349).

"The water drowns ship and sailor..." (*Portable Emerson*, 363).

"Margaret with her radiant genius & fiery heart..." (*Emerson in his Journals*, 540).

88 "everything is free but marriage" (*Emerson: The Mind on Fire*, 331).

"a man's growth is seen..." (*Portable Emerson*, 232).

"if [spouses'] wisdoms come near & meet, there is no danger of passion." (*JMN*, VIII, 392).

90 "You would have me love you..." (*JMN*, VII, 400).

95 "Neither Mrs. Rée in Warmbrunn..." (Binion, Rudolph. *Frau Lou: Nietzsche's Wayward Disciple*. Princeton: Princeton University Press, 1968,).

"I can't live according to some model..." (Andreas-Salomé, Lou. *Looking Back*. Ernst Pfeiffer ed.; Breon Mitchell, trans. New York: Paragon House, 1991, 45-46).

96 "I could consent at most to..."(*Frau Lou*, 49).

"so as to protect you from what people..." (*Frau Lou*, 53).

"raging egoism." (*Frau Lou*, 84).

98 "Your body burns in me..." (Miller, Henry, and Anaïs Nin. *A Literate Passion. Letters of Anaïs Nin and Henry Miller, 1932-1953*. Gunther Stuhlmann, ed. New York: Harcourt Brace Jovanovich, 1987, 269).

99 "God, I hate myself..." (Nin, Anaïs. *Incest*. New York: Harcourt Brace Jovanovich, 1992, 60).

BIBLIOGRAPHY

Allen, Gay Wilson. *Waldo Emerson: A Biography*. New York: Viking, 1991.

Andreas-Salomé, Lou. *Looking Back*. Ernst Pfeiffer ed.; Breon Mitchell, trans. New York: Paragon House, 1991.

Bosco, Ronald A. and Joel Myerson. *The Emerson Brothers: A Fraternal Biography in Letters*. New York: Oxford University Press, 2006.

Binion, Rudolph. *Frau Lou: Nietzsche's Wayward Disciple*. Princeton: Princeton University Press, 1968.

Chevigny, Bell Gale. *Margaret Fuller: The Woman and the Myth*. Boston: Northeastern University Press, 1994.

Chipperfield, Faith. *In Quest of Love: The Life and Death of Margaret Fuller*. New York: Coward McCann, 1957.

Fuller, Margaret. *Portable Margaret Fuller*. New York: Penguin Books, 1994.

———. *The Love-Letters of Margaret Fuller*, 1845-1846. New York : Greenwood Press, 1969.

———. *The Letters of Margaret Fuller*. Robert N. Hudspeth, ed. Ithaca: Cornell University Press, 1983-1994.

———. *Memoirs of Margaret Fuller Ossoli*. Boston: Roberts Brothers, 1881.

Emerson, Ellen Tucker. *One First Love: The Letters of Ellen Louisa Tucker to Ralph Waldo Emerson*. Edith Gregg, ed. Boston: Harvard University Press, 1962.

Emerson, Ralph Waldo. *Journals of Ralph Waldo Emerson*. Vol. VII. A. W. Plumstead and Harrison Hayford, eds. Cambridge: Belknap Press, 1969.

———. *Journals of Ralph Waldo Emerson*. Vol. VII. William Gilman and J. E. Parsons, eds. Cambridge: Belknap Press, 1970.

———. *Letters of Ralph Waldo Emerson*. Rusk, ed. New York: Columbia University Press, 1939.

———. *Portable Emerson*. Carl Bode, ed. New York: Penguin Books, 1981.

Haskins, David Greene. *Ralph Waldo Emerson: His maternal ancestors, with some reminiscences of him*. Port Washington, NY: Kennikat Press, 1971.

Martineau, Harriet. *Society in America*. London: Unders & Otley, 1837.

Miller, Henry, and Anaïs Nin. *A Literate Passion. Letters of Anaïs Nin and Henry Miller, 1932-1953*. Gunther Stuhlmann, ed. New York: Harcourt Brace Jovanovich, 1987.

Nin, Anaïs. *Incest*. New York: Harcourt Brace Jovanovich, 1992.

Pommer, Henry. *Emerson's First Marriage*. Carbondale: Southern Illinois University Press, 1967.

Porte, Joel. *Emerson in his Journals*. Cambridge: Belknap Press, 1982.

INDEX

Alcott, Bronson, 39, 45, 46
American freedom, 3, 5-6, 91, 93-94, 100-101
American Revolution, 22, 32,
Arnim, Bettine von, 42, 43, 50
Barker, Anna, 19, 45; relationship with Sam Ward
de Beauvoir, Simone, 89
Brook Farm, 3, 63
Byron, 15, 24
Carlyle, Thomas, 30, 76, 85
Channing, Ellen, 77, 81
Channing, Ellery, 72, 85, 93
Channing, William, 2
Clarke, James Freeman, 2, 85
The Dial, 47, 74-75
Emerson, Ellen Tucker, 25-31, 37, 55; death, 4, 28-30; relationship with Emerson, 4, 25-30; tuberculosis and, 26, 28
Emerson, Lidian Jackson, 4, 33-37, 38, 40, 48, 65, 68, 69, 70-73; transcendental bible, 40

Emerson, Mary Moody, 22, 28, 29,
Emerson, Ralph Waldo, brothers, 22-26, 27, 30, 31, 38; children, 31, 37, 51, 73; "Circles" (essay), 88; correspondence with Fuller, 5, 43-47, -53-62, 63-68, 69; death and, 4, 22, 25, 27-30, 31, 38, 55, 73, 84, 92, 93; *Divinity School Address*, 38; education, 21-25; "Experience" (essay), 31; family, 21-25, 38; "Fate" (essay), 87; and friendship, 5, 53-62, 63, 64; friendship with Barker, 51-52; friendship with Sturgis, 51-56, 63, 74, 90; friendship with Ward, 47, 51-52; finances, 22, 29-30; inheritance from Ellen's estate, 29-30; lecturing career, 32-33; on marriage, 4, 35, 51, 64,66, 67, 73, 88;

marriage to Ellen Tucker, 4, 25-29; marriage to Lidian Jackson, 4, 33-37, 51, 65, 68, 70-73; meeting Fuller, 20, 41-42; *Nature*, 32, 37; preaching career, 2, 21, 24-26, 29, 30, 48; quarrel with Fuller, 52-62, 63-65, 69, 86-87, 90, 94, 100; relationship with Fuller, 2-6, 41-84, 85-88, 89; "Self-Reliance" (essay), 64; spiritual vision, 23, 29, 30-31; and transcendentalism, 38-39; travels, 30-31, 79; tuberculosis and, 4, 25-28; and writing, 4, 21, 24-25, 74

Everett, Edward, 39

Farrar, Liza, 18-19

Fuller, Hiram, 46

Fuller, Margaret, autobiographical sketch, 8-12; and Bettine von Arnim, 42, 43, 50; childhood, 7-12; and conversation, 8; Conversations, 46-47, 74; death of, 1-2, 84, 93; education, 3, 7-11, 16, 19, 41, 86; and father, 7-9, 11, 12, 14-17, 19, 91; as friend, 14, 15-16, 17-18, 42-, 53-62, 87-88; friendship with Barker, 19, 45, 49, 51-52; friendship with Sam Ward, 19, 45, 50, 51-52,; friendship with Sturgis, 19, 45, 51-52, 78; and Goethe, 15, 17, 42-43; and marriage, 12, 15, 16, 43, 73, 83, 86, 93; marriage of, 1, 80-84; meeting Emerson, 20, 41-42; on mentors, 16-20; mother, 7, 10-11, 82; motherhood, 79, 82; Nino (child), 80-84; pregnancy, 78-79, 92; quarrel with Emerson, 52-62, 63-65, 69, 86-87, 90, 94, 100; relationship with Emerson, 2-6, 41-84, 85-88, 89-90; relationship with Giovanni Ossoli, 76-84; relationship with James Nathan, 75; relationship with Thomas Hicks, 77; rupture with Ward, 50; siblings; socially, 10-14, 15; as teacher, 15, 16, 46-47; travels to Europe, 5, 17, 19, 76, 92; as woman; writings of, 1, 17, 75

Fuller, Timothy, 7; death, 19; political career, 8, 14-15; as teacher, 3, 7-11, 16, 19

German literature and culture, 15, 17, 42
Goethe, 15, 17, 39, 42-43, 50
Greek and Roman culture, 8, 11, 24-25,
Greeley, Horace, 2, 75
Harvard, 23, 24-25
Hedge, Henry, 20, 38
Hicks, Thomas, 77
Hoar, Elizabeth, 38
Italian Revolution, 1, 79-84, 93
Kilshaw, Ellen, 17
Martineau, Harriet, 13, 18-20, 39, 91
Memoirs of Margaret Fuller Ossoli, 2, 5, 41, 85, 86
Mickiewicz, Adam, 76, 85
Miller, Henry, 97-100
Nathan, James, 75
Nietzsche, Elizabeth, 96
Nietzsche, Friedrich, 95-97, 98
Nin, Anaïs, 89, 97-100
Ossoli, Giovanni, 1, 2, 76-84
Rank, Otto, 98
Rée, Paul, 95-96
Rilke, Rainer Maria, 97
Ripley, George, 3, 63
Romanticism (literary), 15, 17, 42
Salomé, Lou, 95-97, 99
Sand, George, 17, 76

Self-reliance, 3, 5-6, 21, 31, 32, 41, 49, 92-93-94, 95, 99, 100-101
Story, Emelyn, 76, 80
Sturgis, Caroline, 19, 45, 51-56, 63, 74, 78, 90
Thoreau Henry David, 3, 39, 84
Transcendental Club, 39-40
Transcendental friendship, 15, 43-62, 63-68, 70-71
Transcendentalism, 38-40, 45
Walden Pond, 3
Ward, Sam, 19, 45, 47, 50, 85; relationship with Anna Barker, 51
Women's lives in the nineteenth century, 2, 7, 10, 12-13, 49, 91